Penguin Books
The Island

Ronald Lockley is well known for his pioneering
studies of birds and other animals. As a young man
he returned to the land of his ancestors to live on
the remote Welsh isle of Skokholm. There he made
his famous studies of the life histories of shearwaters,
petrels, puffins and other sea-birds, and established
the first British bird observatory. It was at Orielton,
a neglected estate in Pembrokeshire, that Ronald
Lockley undertook his classic study *The Private Life
of the Rabbit*. He has pioneered nature reserves in
Britain and abroad, including New Zealand,
where he now lives. In 1977 Ronald Lockley received
an honorary M.Sc. from the University of Wales, in
recognition of his distinction as a naturalist.

His other works include *Shearwaters, Puffins, Grey
Seal, Common Seal, Man Against Nature, Ocean
Wanderers* and *Orielton*, which Penguin is publishing
simultaneously with this volume.

Ronald Lockley

The Island

Illustrated by C. F. Tunnicliffe, R.A.

Penguin Books

Penguin Books Ltd, Harmondsworth,
Middlesex, England
Penguin Books, 625 Madison Avenue,
New York, New York 10022, U.S.A.
Penguin Books Australia Ltd, Ringwood,
Victoria, Australia
Penguin Books Canada Ltd, 2801 John Street,
Markham, Ontario, Canada L3R 1B4
Penguin Books (N.Z.) Ltd, 182–190 Wairau Road,
Auckland 10, New Zealand

First published by André Deutsch Ltd 1969
Published in Penguin Books 1980

Set, printed and bound in Great Britain by
Cox & Wyman Ltd, Reading
Set in Monotype Garamond

For Ann and all who have worked there

Contents

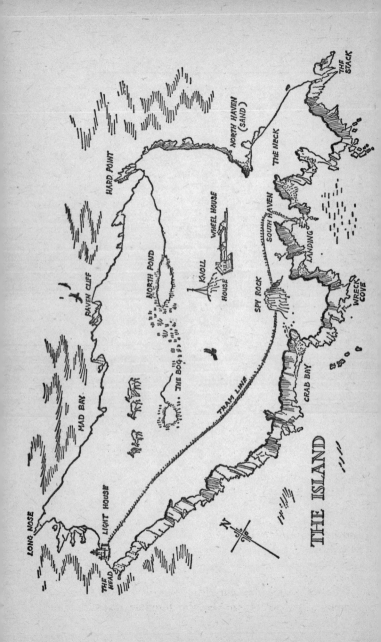

THE ISLAND

LONG NOSE
LIGHT HOUSE
THE HEAD
MAD BAY
RAVEN CLIFF
HARD POINT
NORTH POND
THE BOG
KNOLL
WHEEL HOUSE
HOUSE
SPY ROCK
TRAM LINE
NORTH HAVEN (SAND)
THE NECK
SOUTH HAVEN
LANDING
CRAB BAY
WRECK COVE
THE STACK

N

1 The Discovery

Far away and long ago an island stood, forlorn and deserted by man, alone in the racing tides off the most westerly coast of Wales. Viewed from the mainland through the haze of Atlantic gales which battered its low cliffs the island had the appearance of a huge dismasted ship, a long black hulk with sea-stained superstructure, abandoned to the moods of the winds of heaven which control the storm-waves of the ocean.

When the blue calms and long still sunlight of summer lapped the western sea, the island shone with glowing colours, its sandstone cliffs a deep rose red above the glittering diamonds of the restless inshore currents. Its surface became an enchanting mosaic of flower hues: purple-blue acres of bluebells, delicate flush-pink of the cliff-top thrift, soft yellows of celandine and primrose, snow-white of campion and scurvygrass, vivid greens of grass and fern. Then the island irresistibly stirred the imagination.

At rare intervals in the finest weather, man visited the island, putting a small boat ashore in the one fissure in the cliffs where it was easy to climb up over the rocks. The island was harbourless and too small – a bare 240 acres – to merit permanent settlement. Subject to a twenty-five foot rise and fall of tide it is utterly exposed to the strength of one of the windiest climates in the world. Rooted in the conflicting tidal streams at the entrance to the waterways of the Irish Sea and the Bristol Channel, the island receives the full force of the prevailing westerlies which bring gigantic swells rolling eastwards across four thousand miles of open Atlantic.

Only the ragged young fishermen might stay overnight, tempted by a spell of summer calm, lured by the whirling host of birds, whose nests cover the island plateau and cliffs. Tired of village gossip and home ties the fishermen might luxuriate for a moment in the island's seclusion, enjoying its harvest of sea-birds' eggs, hunting its rabbits, and exploiting its richer fishing returns. But they slept uneasily in their small boats, or amid the cliff flowers close by, ready to sail to the mainland at the first hint of wind.

In 2,000 years of history the little island had not ceased to challenge man, though it would be hard to define the reason precisely. To the older, experienced fisherman it was no longer very remarkable. Accustomed to live by oar and net, lobster-pot and sail, they saw the island with disillusioned eyes at last: to them it was only another lump of land breaking the horizon and the treacherous Atlantic swell five miles from their home beach. When young men fished there in those days of engineless sailboats, they were either more courageous or more foolhardy than their elders who fished nearer home. Courageous because although the catch was better the weather was a greater risk the farther you sailed from overfished home waters. Foolhardy because one day if you persisted you would lose all your gear – pots, nets, and lines – in the sudden storms which brought in the terrible groundsea from the illimitable westward ocean. Then the old men would nod: 'Aye, it always happens!'

But hope is strong in the youth of the heart. The soul of a young man yearns for the horizons beyond experience, the ecstasy to be unlocked over the edge of earth and sea. Hearing the fine tales of adventure related by the old men with sea-weathered eyes and long white beards, I learned that there were giants among them of olden time, whose daring spirit sent them forth to beat the bounds of the world, who rarely returned, but some were heard of as legendary figures, rich in possessions in far countries. A few, a very few, limped home in old age, the bitter secrets of failure hidden under the tawdry glamour of their natural garrulity.

Many a wondrous tale I heard when I first lived in the fishing village, gathering information about the Island. But here my tale is not of man, but of nature within the compass of one small plot of land surrounded by sea, the story of the lonely place to which my particular boyhood daemon at last drove me. Nevertheless, I must perforce describe how I, as a mere man, discovered the island, and came to live there.

*

When I first saw Skokholm, vivid upon the horizon in the windy sunlight of a May evening, I was warned that it was uninhabited, unfarmed, almost inaccessible. But as I had long possessed a natural exhilaration for nature, the sea and solitude, this good news only sang loud within me, to make me restless to sail there. Even before I set foot on it, I was losing my heart to this rock in the ocean.

After two days of waiting for the wind to abate, the young fishermen, whose lobster-pots were set about the island, agreed that the weather might fine off next morning, when they would take friend Harry and me across.

The talkative fisherman said: 'Thee want to go to Skokum? Wunnerful islant, rich, beat anywhere for corn and root crops. Overrun with rabbuts now. Last man to farm it was Bulldog Edwards. Go and see 'im. Lives at Orlandon, a few steps down the road. Particular cuss, my uncle, likes to be asked permission – 'e's still got the lease. Better chat 'im up. Just down the road and over the bridge.'

In remote Wales the natives never tell you it's miles away; that would be discourteous. Keep you happy as long as possible. Life's too short . . . 'Just a few steps' proved to be a four-mile walk. After all, distance is relative.

Many local rumours about Bulldog Edwards. A tight man, they said; and how he had lived obstinately, happily, unconventionally with a pretty housekeeper on the Island. Robust still, with flowing white beard, a belligerent eye, wind-wrinkled skin and a voice not without the singing larks of Skokholm still in its soft drawl. His talk was old-fashioned and quiet, as with resignation.

'Ah, Skokum! Now that's an islant for thee. Thee'll like 'un if thee likes the burrds. I ought'n never to have left 'un. Peaceful as 'eaven. But the dratted war came. Aye, 'elp thyself – if thee can get there. Come and tell me afterwards.'

Another windy night of waiting to cross. Harry and I slept in his car at Trehill Farm, opposite the island. The farm girls put flowers, toys, lavender and pennies in my stockings which

I had washed and hung out to dry. They wanted to flirt and be courted adventurously by these strangers to their treeless, wind-torn peninsula. Provoking, pretty, hilarious, tied to dairy calves and cackling geese throughout the procreative year, they were simply happy in healthy young womanhood. But my dream was inward, secret, shy, concerned with islands, birds and a hope of solitude and peace in which to study wild nature.

Dead calm next morning. It took two hours for the fishermen to row the sailing boat *Foxtrot* over a current-swirled blue sea to the ruby sandstone cliffs of Skokholm. All the time Jim, hirsutely dark, handsome, lean, tall, talked his head off, garrulous as a jay; but Jack, fair, ugly, plump, short, was silent. Ideal fishing mates: the first careless, rash, foolish; the other steady, thoughtful, reserved.

We glided to the landing-place in the south-facing opening in the rocks, watched by a reception committee of a thousand puffins strolling on the flower-strewn slopes, bowing silently to each other, rubbing painted beaks together, or merely staring vacantly around. Red-billed oystercatchers piped a loud welcome, and gulls swooped anxiously from scores of nests in the cliffs. Flowers, flowers, everywhere – a rock garden of surpassing loveliness.

'Must paint this landing-place!' gasped Harry the artist. 'Colour quite unbelievable!'

My own heart was thumping wildly. We walked the hundred yards to a tumbledown cottage slowly, savouring every step. Another deputation – this time of a thousand brown-bodied beasts – ringed us at a discreet distance: rabbits staring but mute on their lawns of smooth grass along the edge of green bracken under the stone-banked earth walls of a little meadow. A blackbird fluted from the chimney of the broken house. Larks sang full-throated overhead. On a rocky knoll behind the old farm buildings a trio of seapies (oystercatchers) skirled a lament, heads bowed as if ashamed of these ragged men interrupting the idyll of their island life.

I was tongue-tied, with a choking sensation of joy. I wanted to shout my delight. Coming up behind us the talkative fisherman called out: 'Rabbuts – you wait till dusk – thousands come out, and thousands of cocklollies with 'em. Every burrow in the ground 'as a dozen of each!'

Bursting into the cottage he flung his canvas hold-all upon a wide driftwood-built bed which half-filled the living-room. Cosy aroma of cut plug tobacco, rotten eggs, soot, stale clothes and mice . . . 'Millions of mice,' Jim said, 'but no rats. Want some fresh eggs? I'll show thee; bring a bag and follow me.'

He flung some stale gulls' eggs through a hole in the window, startling two puffins making love, nose to nose, at the entrance to their burrow in the garden wall, their feet pattering upon a carpet of sweet scented sea-campion.

Over the level plateau peewits wailed above the long molinia grass, audibly winnowing their black pinions as they dived upon us. Jim's long legs swung from one gull's nest to another. Three-egg clutches he squelched with his fisherman's clogs. Only the one- or two-egg clutches were fresh. He filled a basket with these, and pursued his destructive course over the sloping cliff. He collected the huge pear-shaped eggs of the guillemots and razorbills in the tumbled rocks.

We left him and wandered over the beautiful plateau. From the top of the high point, Spy Rock, we could see the whole island as a map, stretching about a mile's length from north-east to south-west, and half a mile wide at its greatest breadth. The wandering coast-line could perhaps be six miles, in and out, all cliff. The map in my pocket gave the highest point as 175 feet above the sea, the acreage as 242. The plateau itself rose gently from fifty feet in the north-east to over a hundred feet in the south-west. Fresh water was trapped in a marshy central plain, where we could see two substantial ponds. A procession of gulls bathed here, washing the salt off their plumage. The eastern half of the island was laid out in little fields, alive now with rabbits; encroaching bracken and heather provided cover for huge colonies of nesting gulls, and smaller birds. Strangely, although the sea-birds excited me to rapture, my heart was moved almost as much by the sight of familiar lesser birds singing and nesting: sedge-warblers, pied wagtails, swallows, stonechats, wheatears, and the homely hedge-sparrows or dunnocks.

As dusk fell the birds were almost silent. From the bushes

by the spring at the foot of the meadow, as I was drawing water, the sedge-warbler again burst forth into rich bubbling mimetic music. In the calm air the song could be heard even inside the cottage, where the fishermen were finishing their supper of gulls' eggs.

'Listen! Did thee know we 'ad the nightingale 'ere? Listen to 'im!' said the talkative one. 'Comes every year to Skokum, don't 'im, Jack?'

No answer. Jack is a gentleman, too polite to call Jim a liar in front of us, for he has discovered by our conversation that we are mad about birds, and to him we are therefore authorities on them.

'An' the water in the Skokum spring comes all the way from the top of the Presely Mountains, thirty miles away. Aye, Jack?' Jim sprawled on the bed, boots and all.

'Ah.' Still essentially polite, the cautious Jack utters the one safe ambiguous answer, neither yes nor no. He surely must be a natural-born scientist. Every golden moment of his silence pleases me. As proof of his gentlemanly habits Jack takes off his boots before lying down. His snores are presently wholesome, untroubled.

By the light of our storm-lantern Harry and I are each reading a volume of the only literature we have found on a shelf in the room: a huge family Bible, full octavo size, four inches thick, bound in two parts.

It is quite dark outside. Jim sleeps lightly, wakes, pokes the driftwood fire into life, surprised to find us still present, and inevitably talks.

'Valuable old thing, that Bible. Been in the family four hundred years.'

'It's dated 1763,' says Harry, who is a keen collector of antiques.

'Aye, very very old. Nice condition though,' yawns Jim. 'What's it worth?'

'Is it for sale?' Harry is alert, scenting a bargain. 'Who does it belong to?'

'Me,' says Jim, with a flickering uneasy glance at the unconscious Jack. 'Old Bulldog's fancy woman brought it 'ere twenty-five years ago. She was religious, but now she's dead; and they say poor old Bulldog's got cancer. I'm 'is nearest male heir. D'you wanna buy it? Everything on the islant's mine now . . .'

'It's not doing much good in this salt air. Look, some of the leaves are stuck with mildew. What d'you want for it?'

'H'm. Coupla quid?'

'You can keep it – at that price, and lugging it around until I get home. I live more'n a hundred miles from here.'

'Gimme what it's worth to thee, then. I doan like seeing it rot away – like thee says.'

'Alright. I'm willing to take it away for five bob.'

A cynical laugh from Jim, who changes the subject for a while. He talks again of the cocklollies (shearwaters) which will, any minute now, come screaming around the cottage, millions of them, homing to their underground burrows. I long for this event. I go out into the pitch-dark night to listen. Faint noises from drowsy gulls only. No stars, a cloud bank has swallowed the dome of heaven. When I come back, the bargaining is almost concluded. Jack is still snoring blissfully.

'Thee's tough,' Jim is saying. 'I wunna sell for less than ten bob.'

'No, that's a lot of money these days.'

(And so it was; in fact at that time more than the average day's pay for a labourer.)

'Split the difference?'

'No! I might give you six bob.'

'It's a deal at seven!'

'Oh, alright.' Harry's show of reluctance compels my admiration. He loves a good haggle.

*

At intervals during the day Harry and I had heard a cooing half-strangled sound issuing from the innumerable rabbit-burrows. Now we eagerly strolled into the darkness, flashing the lantern here and there, over burrows from which the weird songs issued in growing strength. Suddenly the blood-curdling cry seemed to rush straight at us, as its author plumped down from the sky towards our light.

There it was, the black and white bird, as large as a pigeon, which I was soon to know so well, sitting on the turf, waddling a few steps, then vanishing into a burrow. Presently a duet issued, as the mated birds discussed their affairs under the earth with unearthly cackles.

One, two, soon tens, then hundreds, and by midnight thousands of cocklollies arrived from the ocean. Their crowing vibrated to a crescendo from every quarter of the island, above and below ground. How can I describe it? At times it seemed to be a long-drawn sob of human agony, at others a deafening concert of witches, burning at the stake. Usually a triple crowing, followed by a longer wail. Every step after midnight needed to be with care. These long-winged albatross-like birds seemed helpless on land, unable to walk properly, not moving from our path. We blundered into them, they into us, underfoot and on the wing.

Estimating populations of burrow-nesting animals is difficult at any time, but for the sake of modifying the wild figure of Jim Fisherman's 'millions of cocklollies', we provisionally reckoned these birds must be in the five-figure bracket, say 20,000 adult breeding shearwaters.

Trying to count the puffins had amused us during the day. These underground nesters had paraded in their thickest numbers along the cliff-tops early in the evening. They sat about in groups comically like gossiping frock-coated red-nosed pigmy men, on every rock outcrop, some far inland, even – a few – on the dilapidated roof of the cottage. By making sample counts of groups over sections of the island, we had already arrived at the same comfortable round figure of 20,000 – but this time, *pairs*. It seemed incredible – could there be 20,000 shearwaters and 40,000 puffins on Skokholm! Yet our estimates were surely conservative? In addition there were, of course, the gulls, probably a total of 1,500 pairs of the three species: herring, lesser and greater black-backed gulls.

And the rabbits? How did they cope with this invasion of their burrows by 60,000 shearwaters and puffins? Jim Fisherman had said that 5,000 rabbits was reckoned the usual catch each winter. Even allowing for his notorious powers of exaggeration, to produce even half this number for export, there must be a total of 5,000 rabbits, all ages, in summer inhabiting the burrows with the 60,000 birds. We did some simple arithmetic. Allowing the island to be 240 acres, and allowing each pair of birds one burrow each, there would be around 125 burrows to each acre, which is roughly one bird burrow to each thirty-nine square yards of surface. It could very well be many more, since some dry parts of the island had a burrow hole to the square yard, but of course the wet central marsh had none. Room for all then, surprisingly; but who decided which burrow?

Thrusting an arm down some of the shallower burrows I received a severe peck from an indignant nesting shearwater or puffin. Looking at my bleeding fingers I decided that the rabbit must come last in the peck-order of dominance below ground.

At dusk the puffins had gone to sleep below ground, one by one disappearing through their flowery doorways. Occasionally as we strolled around, almost deafened by the shearwater chorus, we heard a sleepy puffin yawn audibly: 'Ahr! Har! Har!' from its nest deep in the ground, as it brooded its huge round, faintly speckled egg.

A soft purring sound in the night air began, gentle notes on the bass woodwind, pipes of Pan from among and above the broken rocks in the cliffs, and from the holes between the stones of the old hedge-walls. Other nocturnal birds are here – dainty Mother Carey's Chickens. In the ring of lantern light we glimpsed swallow-sized birds flitting past, humming a tiny song, and visible chiefly from the white rump which danced like a will-o'-the-wisp hither and thither. Those charming birds – the stormy petrels of the mariner – fluttered and squeezed into the smallest holes to join their partner on the single fragile egg laid on bare earth. Ear to the crevices I could hear a purring connubial conversation; while my nose detected the strong, musky, petrel smell.

'Me-dee-arr! Me-dee-arr!' A trilling note of deep excitement, interrupted at intervals with a sharp hiccup of joy, as if one bird had nibbled the other unexpectedly in the pitch darkness.

'Harry! Harry! Listen to the storm-petrels . . . why, there's dozens in these old hedges!'

'It's the Arabian Nights' Entertainment, all over again, but much more satisfying!'

'Harry?'

'Yes?'

'I want to spend the whole summer here! I want to live here forever. D'you suppose . . . do you think I . . .'

2 Possession

To dwell alone and simply upon a small island of my own, to study its wild life intimately, had been my version of every boy's fleeting ambition to emulate Robinson Crusoe, to be one of the Swiss Family Robinson. Why it should have become, after school days, my most burning desire I cannot tell, any more than one can explain our stranger daemon within, which drives adult man to climb a mountain wall, to sail the ocean single-handed, to plant a wood, to travel to Tibet, to create a garden. My particular genius sought to surround me with the beautiful forms of the birds, wild flowers and other living creations of nature, away from the artificiality of man's con-urbial life. Hence I had turned as soon as possible to live on the land, and blessed with very little capital, I had become a small farmer. For I was no book scholar. I had abandoned school at seventeen to graduate in natural history (without the aid of a tutor or academic books) in the university of the fields and woods of rural Monmouthshire. Each summer holiday had found me searching for the island I still dreamed of.

It could not be true that I had at last discovered it? I was astounded and delighted, and fearful, when we returned from Skokholm, to find that Bulldog Edwards was prepared to resign his lease to me if I paid him for the forthcoming winter crop of island rabbits. As he spoke, the old man praised the island in extravagant terms, once more regretting he was too old to live there.

'Be thou going to live on Skokum this winter? I'll recommend thee a good rabbut-trapper . . .'

It was a direct challenge to put my dreams into effect, to exchange the theory of armchair adventures for the physical reality of the fight with approaching winter and rough weather, with the upheaval of selling my little farm and changing my secure, comfortable mainland way of life for a precarious existence upon an exposed plateau in the ocean, on an island about which I knew almost nothing. At the age of twenty-three, dare I risk such a move?

Yes, I was full of little fears, let me admit; while a song of triumph hammered in my brain. I knew I would not be happy until I secured the island somehow for my very own.

I must find out everything I could. The landlord's agent was a cautious old man, but took my application as seriously as I did. He produced deeds and old maps, and told me all he could about Skokholm. This was not very much. Reading between the lines it was clear that sooner or later the sea and weather had defeated every previous tenant. There were breaks in the tenancies during which only cattle and sheep were in occupation, the little farmhouse and its buildings abandoned. The biggest income of late years had been the rabbit crop.

In the days of negotiating a new lease which followed I explored the archives of the local library and museum for the story of man's fugitive connections with the island.

Islands close to the mainland, such as Skomer and Gateholm, it seemed, had considerable visible archaeological remains, proving a first occupation at least 2,000 years ago. Thus on Gateholm (accessible at low tide from the mainland) numerous hut-circles exist, and from some of these sites archaeologists had recovered brooches and coins contemporary with the Roman occupation of Britain. But on isolated Skokholm there were no signs of these homes and settlements characteristic of the Iron Age.

Local history records the ravages of the Vikings on this coast. Their ships were wintered (eighth century) in Milford Haven, where they established settlements by driving out the native Welsh. Many place-names of Scandinavian origin have remained ever since. The islands all have Norse names: Skomer (originally *Scalmey*, meaning the Cloven Island), Ramsey (possibly Hrafn's Island, meaning Raven's Island), Grassholm (the Green Islet). 'Ey' is Norse for Island, and 'Holm' means Islet.

Skokholm is variously spelt in old documents, most often as *Stok-* or *Skok*-holm. The prefixes could have been derived from the Scandinavian 'Skokkr', meaning a trunk of wood, a chest or a ship's hulk; or from 'Stokkr', a sound or seaway. Whether it was so named by the Viking marauders because it looked like a huge hulk, or had stores of wood or timber, even driftwood; or whether it was to them simply the Islet in the Sound, we may never know. Both derivations might be appropriate. Skokholm could even have been a wooded island at that time, for there were no rabbits to destroy sapling trees until the Normans introduced these rodents several centuries later.

I was to unravel the fascinating story of the rabbits and the Normans in due course.

*

Skokholm has a glowing red rock. I knew nothing of its geology, but I read the details of a survey which indicated that the whole island is composed of a series of beds of Old Red Sandstone, laid down under Armorican seas millions of years ago. During many centuries the bedrock lay, now under water, now under ice. There were long warm periods when the ice-caps of our planet shrank under a fiery mood of the life-giving sun, causing the oceans to rise and drown the edges of the shifting continents. The crust of earth just here lay close beneath water running to and fro under the tug of sun and moon pulling together or in opposition. From mountains high above Armorican seas tropical rains and winds eroded the ancient mother rocks and lavas. Roaring rivers ground boulders to pebbles, and pebbles to sand. In the shallows of delta and estuary fine-grained beds of detritus were deposited around islands of older rock. Waves and currents smoothed the moving grains into level layers of coarse and fine mudstone and sandstone, leaving ripple marks which can be detected today.

Carrying the book of the survey with me, I returned to the island for one quick visit in August. I read how, in arid periods, long before primitive man paddled his canoe there, the shallow water had evaporated, laying down limy deposits, which survive today in the form of tiny marl-like pellets, whitish with calcium carbonate. I could examine these curious ellipsoids, formed in delta days, for they are the first to weather out under salt spray when the surface is exposed, leaving the red matrix of Skokholm with its present character-istic pitted appearance. Yes, that was obvious enough – the rock was mighty sharp underfoot!

During succeeding aeons (I read) the newly formed sand-stone was uplifted above the sea by earth pressures which dis-torted the sedimentary layers, and altered the bedding angles with fold and cleavage. Thus was born the island. But the elements had not quite finished polishing it. They never will. All is flux and change even in the slow world of geology.

On the surface of Skokholm lie scattered many large stones and boulders which have no connection with the sandstone. I was astonished to learn that the Pleistocene ice sheet had once ground its way over the land, and when it melted it left behind boulder clay and some huge alien rocks. These erratics are now covered with lichen. I scratched them and found the beautiful colours of the original rock – bright green, and white. The experts say these boulders have probably travelled south from Scotland, on their unimaginable journey of half a thousand miles encased in glacial ice, at the rate of a few yards a year!

Reading its romantic geological history, I knew unexpec-tedly, gladly, that I was not going to live on a lump of dead rock in the ocean but with my feet upon a living, ever-changing soil and stone of fascinating provenance, above red rocks that delighted the eye, and upreared strata that filled the mind with wonder. Marvellous, too, were the many uses which I should make of the island's mineralogy: clay for building, for pond making, perhaps for pottery; sandstone for roof tiles, shell sand for concreting, and for sweetening the garden; boulders and gravelly deposits for wall-making.

The boulder-clay deposited over the central plateau of the island holds water as a valuable reservoir against the droughts of summer, for it impedes drainage. The winter rains seep but slowly downhill, until, trapped by the faults in the sandstone beneath, the clarified water issues forth in a series of pure, never-failing springs along the eastern side, convenient for man, his livestock and wild creatures at the foot of the little enclosed fields. In summer former inhabitants cut peaty turf from this boggy centre of the island, providing slow-burning winter fuel.

This was my new home! An island entirely ringed by low red cliffs rising between fifty and one hundred feet high, with inland crags up to 170 feet above sea level. Much of the sandstone has been heaved and folded from its original level plane, especially on the north coast where it is often nearly perpendicular. The sea can more easily tear apart upended strata, eating into the land and forming the present northern bays; huge slabs of pink rock are flung down at the foot of the cliffs, to be smashed by the ground swells of winter storms. In summer the sea-birds find nesting places in the labyrinth of the upper talus.

Book in hand, I continued my geological exploration. The bedding planes are more level on the south side of the island, presenting a sheer resistant face to the storms which assault from that direction. Rising from deeper water, this solid red wall is picturesquely veined with wide greenish-grey marly layers, and narrow lines of crystal glittering in sunlight. These southern cliffs look handsome from seaward, but having few ledges are not hospitable to nesting birds. On one central crag, high above the tide-races, I flushed the lordly peregrine falcon, as he rested, gazing over the Atlantic, waiting upon his appetite to stoop at puffin or pigeon, or other passing prey.

I followed the falcon's gaze to the huge open Atlantic southwards. While I had been quietly geologizing, the weather had changed; clouds and rain showers were sweeping swiftly up from south. In a few moments steep waves began to break upon the landing steps. The fishermen called me to leap in as they manoeuvred the *Foxtrot* close to the rocks. It was an exciting get-away, but at last the sail was hoisted and we raced north on the flowing tide.

The tide! If I could wonder at the vivid story of the living rock and soil of Skokholm revealed to me between the formidable wordage and scientific terms of the geologists, how much more was I to be excited by observing and comprehending the tremendous tidal streams in whose path the island lay? Next to the tides of the Bay of Fundy and the Gulf of St Malo, those of the Severn Sea are the most powerful in the world. At spring tide (new and full moons) the sea rises twenty-five feet above the low water line. Thus an immense volume of water forces its way past the island, racing north at the moment of high tide at about six miles an hour, swifter than any small boat can sail; and south at the same speed over low water. It changes direction at each half-tide, that is, just over each six hours.

I had already learned from the fishermen how the configuration of the coast affected the flow of the tides, how essential it was to sail at the favourable moment – 'the first of the tide' – when the current was gentle and moving in the right direction. But much depended on the strength of the wind. Even a light breeze blowing against a strong tidal stream produced a nasty short sea too steep for a small boat.

How magnificent was the living sea about the island! I was to admire every mood of the never-still waters, now deep blue in calms, now snow-white in storms. In due course, I was gradually to learn the reasons for each changing facet of the swirling, racing currents, their colour, speed, direction, and every movement inspired by their masters, the winds, the moon and the sun. I was to learn the apt local name of each of the scores of jagged rocks and sea-smoothed reefs, which diverted the tides, causing dangerous – sometimes useful – eddies.

When the full spring tides, driven before a southerly gale – as on that August day – roared at high water into the opening in the rocks which by courtesy was marked South Haven on the map, spray and foam flew over the top of the island from crashing breakers. The cliff would tremble under me as I lay flat upon the grass. At high water ton-weight boulders groaned as they were levered into new positions by the doubled strength of a rebounding wave and used as battering-rams to break down more of the land.

The majesty of the sea was a joy. Storms were never to dismay me. My inquisitive mind ever sought to understand, as it marvelled at the strength and beauty of the elementary forces of nature so starkly contending around me. Even as the island had been born of material gathered by marine forces, and by earth movement and erosion, had become a detached portion of the wave-cut platform which forms the southern portion of the mainland peninsula of Pembrokeshire, so it was now being worn down each day by the strength of its maternal source, the sea, as a mother slowly and surely destroys the child she clasps too long in her arms. Already she had torn away the north-east point of the island, and formed the islet of the Stack. Next, in perhaps 5,000 years – a second of geological time – she would wear through the fissure of South Haven, and send her tides racing into the sandy slit of North Haven, over the present isthmus which is barely sixty yards wide. The island would slowly vanish below the sea? And be overlaid with new sandstone detritus? Unless another glacial age approached, to lower the level of ocean? Unless the drowned crust of mother earth once more swelled, buckled and pushed the island upwards, raising her beaches far from the tireless power of the sea?

This was the lonely, beautiful, exciting island which awaited my hope of living there.

*

Suddenly, after months of anxious negotiation, all obstacles were overcome. The lease was mine, for an almost nominal rent of £26 a year. It stated in quaint but satisfying phraseology that I was entitled to the 'peaceful possession and quiet enjoyment' of the island, and I had an option to buy it within two years – at a price I could not afford. I sold what I owned of my little farm – the stock and goodwill – to another young man. I moved my few sticks of furniture and my dilapidated second-hand car a hundred miles across Wales to the fishing village opposite the island. It was October. The car was old. What I needed was a boat. I sold the car to augment my slender capital which I had transferred to the local bank.

But how to begin? I told myself that all I needed was shelter sufficient for a night roost and to house my few books. For the rest I was young enough to acquire skill in making a plain living from the products of the island and the sea around it. I had neither the capital nor the inclination to burden myself with my late profession of small farming, of raising domestic animals, of tilling the land for market crops. Others had struggled to do this, on a grander scale farming the island, laboriously dividing the surface into fields with once neat, but now tumbled-down, earth hedges walled with the small red stones,

27

laid herring-bone fashion. It was sad to see these protective hedge-banks, laid with such care, much torn down by burrowing rabbits; but at least the storm-petrels had found safe homes in the small crevices, and hundreds of puffins were utilizing the holes dug by the rabbits.

Those pioneer island farmers had lived their dreams, and one by one vanished; their posterity had not wished to continue the fight with wind and sea and isolation. The lesson was plain, could I but read it. But I had long decided that, like Thoreau, I would be content to carry off the harvest without the aid of a wheelbarrow. Every moment of leisure would be devoted to my main love, the study of birds.

Yes, my needs would be small. Perforce a small boat to fish with, to pay rare visits to the mainland with such natural produce as I could muster for sale – rabbits, lobsters and crabs – to pay for my few simple requirements unobtainable on the island. For the rest, I would want only a few hand tools with which to restore the cottage farmhouse, and cultivate the little walled garden.

Late in October I engaged the silent fisherman Jack, ten years older and wiser than I, as boatman and handyman. As it proved, I could not have found a better helpmate, fearless, loyal, sweet-mouthed with soft words and silence. On his advice I bought a second-hand boat, sixteen and a half feet long: little more than a shallow dinghy she was, but light enough to be rowed, and – most essential – hauled up on the island. The inboard motor proved unreliable, but Jack cut an ash mast from the local copse, and sewed a fine sail (which was more than once to save our lives in sudden storms), and dyed it red. I was ready to occupy Skokholm.

Local fishermen, their boats drawn high up for the winter, shook their heads. Behind my back they prophesied that I would soon retreat whence I had come, defeated by the weather which had driven away every other pioneer. To my face the villagers politely wished me well; but, as day after day the autumnal gales raged into November, they told more tales of drowning, of wrecks and other disasters which had befallen those island pioneers. At night, listening by their hospitable kitchen fires in the cottages – for at that moment I had nowhere else to sleep – I laughed exultantly in my heart, with no thought other than the hope that the weather would be calm enough on the morrow for us to cross to my new, exciting home.

Home! When at last I could reach it, what a rough and pitiable shelter it was – now that I can look back upon that first winter of incessant storms! But I did not think so then. The rusted sheet iron nailed over the holes in the cottage roof frequently blew off as the gales roared through the broken doors and windows. Even the solid stone walls quivered in sudden savage squalls. On such nights we crouched before a spitting fire of driftwood, wrapped in greatcoats to shield ourselves from the howling draughts. The silent Jack, tranquil as ever, rolled cigarettes, sewed the sail, made tea, and presently went to bed, fully clothed; and at last, pleasantly tired with planning the glorious future, I followed suit, throwing my oilskin stormcoat over my bunk. The rain which ended each storm would inevitably drip upon me through the patched-up roof.

On calm nights we went out to hunt rabbits with torch and gun. Then, before turning in, I would stroll alone over the beautiful land, lit by stars or moon. I still lived with wonder at my good fortune in possessing such a home, where every moment of day and night was vivid with bird movement and cries, with singing wind and running tide. Invariably I walked down to the South Haven, and gazed through the dusk of night to catch the reflected light from the sea. If a piece of driftwood had come in, I climbed down and collected it. My little boat *Storm-Petrel* was safely hauled up above the storm line by the handwinch we had fixed in the creek there, above a tiny beach of rose-red pebbles. Safe and peaceful; and I could think clearly of the future. My plans were crystallizing.

First I engaged another man to help Jack trap the rabbits. I myself began to restore the roof of the one building which had resisted the gales better than the cottage itself; this was the barn, a solid stone rectangle with an ancient threshing floor of wide red flagstones. Its roof had stood firm because of the weight of the heavy sandstone tiles dug from a quarry on the island; but it was sagging now, and one corner had been ripped wide open.

I must repair the barn in order to live in it. Then, early in the spring, I should strip the roof and interior of the cottage completely, and spend next summer rebuilding it as snug and comfortable as Bulldog Edwards had once boasted it had been – twenty years ago. With the cottage restored, the barn would be a general storehouse for the fishing gear, lobster-pots and other impedimenta of island life. Jack talked seldom, but when he did his theme was most often of the wonderful fishing for lobsters, crayfish and crabs for which Skokholm waters were famous. In spare moments he began to weave lobster-pots, using withies he collected ashore on our period-ical visits to market the rabbits.

All the sea-birds had flown, save a few gulls and the resident oystercatchers. But many other birds had arrived. From my elevated position on the roof of the barn, as day after day, with unskilled fingers, I fitted new rafters and battens cut from driftwood planks, and laid upon these heavy tiles, I enjoyed and studied the winter movements of the birds out of the corner of one eye. Nevertheless that very act of faith – the restoration of a building erected maybe 200 years ago – compelled my inward thoughts away from the vivid present scene to those forgotten men who had laboured here. I began to see more clearly that the last pioneer – Bulldog Edwards – had been a man after my own heart, to have lasted a dozen or more years here out of love for Skokholm. There was evidence of his work, though the winds had torn down the roofs he had repaired, the bracken and rabbits had reconquered the garden he and his woman had tended so successfully, and the heather was spreading over the field he knew as The Green, where (he had said) turnips as big as footballs had been raised. Collecting stones and tiles fallen from the roofless farm buildings, I discovered rusted tools, old millstones and even copper coins dated a hundred years ago. Who were the first house-builders here?

These relics pleased me. Of course the early settlers had needed a corn-mill, to grind the home-grown wheat and barley. They had needed to be self-supporting – even more than I must be. One day I must uncover the whole story of man's settlement here, perhaps learn the name of the islander who laid the foundation stones of the house and the farm buildings.

'"Tis said,' the trapper Dick reminisced one evening, 'that them two big stone jambs [gate posts] to the farm yard do mark the graves of an old couple who died on the island many long years ago, long afore Captain Harrison's time, long afore Bulldog's time it were. In their ole age them two wudden never go ashore. They ask'd to be buried on Skokum. 'Tis true, they do say.'

But soon I had evidence of a much older occupation. On the surface of the low eastern peninsula of the Neck I found flint flakes scratched from the earth by rabbits. Local geology will not admit flint as native to Pembrokeshire, therefore (said the archaeologist who examined my specimens) the island must have been visited by the Mesolithic people – perhaps on temporary hunting forays – whose presence on the mainland opposite is proved by flint chipping sites there. This is so far back, around 8,000 BC, that Skokholm had probably not yet been separated from the mainland – at that date England was still part of the mainland of Europe, and the Rhine and Thames were tributaries of the same river system.

All that winter, while the storms buffeted the island, sending a mist of spray drifting continuously across it so that my lips were salt each day, while I struggled to re-roof the barn between maintenance duties of cooking, baking bread, washing clothes, recording wild life, I sought to unravel the history of the builders of these walls and once neat hedges. The old rabbit-catcher Dick was deaf, and as uncommunicative as Jack. He could not read or write but he remembered the names of some of the nineteenth-century family Harrison who had been the last bona fide farmers, ploughing the fields and keeping a dairy. On rare visits ashore I obtained local history books from the county library, and the landlord's agent allowed me to copy from the old deeds in his possession.

Yet still I could find nothing recorded between the Stone Age people, and the naming of the island by the Vikings. No sign of the Romano-British period so obvious in grass-grown defensive earthworks and the foundations of living quarters still clearly visible along the mainland coast opposite and at Skomer Island, just two miles to the north.

Skomer, over 800 acres, and easy of access from the mainland, rich in pasturage and sea-birds, with an excellent harbour, must have been coveted for settlement, as the numerous remains of ancient field systems, stone-walled houses, folds and enclosures – outside the more modern central farm – testify. From a close study of these outward signs, which include a promontory fort or cliff castle earthwork of Iron Age date, it is clear to the archaeologist that Skomer had been settled at least as far back as the first century before Christ.

Surrounded by fierce tide-races at that time, as today, Skokholm's plateau of 240 acres was less desirable. Evidently it had remained inviolate down into historic times, save for occasional brief, fine weather forays to collect its sea-birds, and perhaps the produce of introduced sheep and goats.

At last I stumbled on what must be the first reference in print to the island – earlier in history than I had dared hope. This was an undated charter (now in the British Museum) by which William Marshal the Younger, Earl of Pembroke 1219–31, grants to a certain Gilbert de Vale 1,500 acres of land and a mill in Ireland in exchange for lands in Pembrokeshire which included the island of 'Scugholm'. This exchange meant that Earl William and his four brothers all held the island as private property in turn; but all died young, without male heirs. The extensive possessions of the Earls (originally seized by conquest of the native Welsh) passed to their sisters (co-heirs) and were divided up, Skokholm falling to the Bohun line. In the Calendar of Close Rolls is a document dated 22 June 1275 at Westminster ordering the bailiff of Kermerdyn (Carmarthen) to cause Humphrey de Bohun (the Seventh, and Earl of Hereford) to have 'seisin of the island of Stokhom' as part of his inheritance on the death in that year of his grandfather Humphrey, the Fifth of that name.

Gilbert de Vale (or de la Vall in one document – no doubt he took his name as was customary in Norman times from the land he occupied in a small vale or valley, now called Dale, on the mainland opposite Skokholm) is shown in various documents to have been an important local landholder. He was Seneschal of Pembroke 1241–6. On the death of the last Earl Marshal of Pembroke in 1247, the feodary of the Earl's possessions included land in or near Dale held by Gilbert de Vale by the render of feudal services pertaining to half a knight's fee (that is, he was the tenant) of the Earl and the Earl's heirs. He also held the land in Ireland, mentioned in the last paragraph, which he had exchanged for other lands and the island of Skokholm in Pembrokeshire. The point is that the de Vale family no longer held Skokholm, which had remained the private property of the Earl.

From the upper windows of the present Dale Castle it is possible to see Skokholm four miles away in the western sea, and there is no doubt that the squire de Vale – nearest resident feudal landholder – was in a strong position to exploit the island. In the legal confusion over the extent of the estates of the demised Earls Marshal and their Bohun heirs, the de Vale family continued – illicitly – to enjoy the revenue from Skokholm (variously spelt by the Norman scriveners: the few who could read or write in medieval times often could not spell correctly) for some fifty years after they had yielded the island to their feudal overlord the Earl Marshal.

The old documents are in Latin. On my rare visits to London I could handle, and with help translate, some of them at the Public Records Office and other archives. How fortunate it was that they had been so well preserved on vellum and parchment, on the finely drawn skin of calf and sheep – complete with their heavy wax seals. For I was to learn from them why this remote little Welsh island had been so important to the descendants of the Norman barons, as well as the reason for the preservation of these ancient deeds in the custody of the Crown.

Nevertheless my readers may not be so fascinated by my summary of the contents of these documents, as they affect Skokholm. I shall not be surprised therefore, if they skip this purely historical part – which I have placed in the Appendix at the end of this book.

3 Winter

An extract from my diary that winter:

January 2nd. Heavy swell breaking on the South Haven landing beach after yesterday's storm. We failed to launch the *Storm-Petrel* at half-flood, the boulders and the sea too rough; so tried again when the tide was high enough to fill the creek. Got clear, after a few ticklish moments expecting the sea to fling us on to the sharp rocks. The Gods were unkind, however – first, the engine would not start; second, there was a lively sea with small waves dashing inboard as we loaded the rabbits and rowed out into the wind; third, the nor'west wind came in squalls, heeling the boat over so that we shipped green water, as we flew before the storm, one man bailing, the other watching the sail. Just as we were crossing above the Cable Rock in Jack Sound, the current swirled us around and the yard snapped in twain! The cool Jack nimbly rolled the canvas up as we leaped to the oars. Finally we had to get the loaded boat, somehow, through a heavy surf pounding on Martinshaven beach!

The storm suddenly eased enough for us to return at 5 p.m. We sailed gloriously by moonlight, and the magic of that passage home was worth all the troubles of the day. Later I walked alone around the whole island coast, singing aloud. When I reached South Haven, to bid my brave little boat goodnight, the sea in that magic harbour was silver with moonlight. My exhilaration needed cooling and I threw off my clothes and plunged twice into the calm glistening water! Then once more to stride over the island – this time through the centre, to listen to the cries of snipe, and the gabbling of the wild duck on the pond.

Despite the several disasters of the boat half-swamped in bad weather during crossings which I forced Jack to make against his better judgement – for I was impatient and ignorant, and he tolerant and lion-hearted; despite the damage this and the beaching of the boat in heavy seas caused to the *Storm-Petrel*; despite weeks of storm when we could not cross to market the rabbits, my only source of income; despite the trickling away of my slender capital in purchases of boat and equipment, wages, food, and items for the repair of the island cottage, as well as for the building of a small hut with sleeping bunks on a site above the mainland beach at Martinshaven (an essential refuge for an islander awaiting calm weather to cross home, as well as a store place for post and goods); despite all these hazards, I survived that first winter with no thought of failure or retreat.

Instead all day long there was a song of joy in my heart, a deep excitement which made me record spontaneously in my diary: 'I am very happy here!' 'This is a marvellous place!' 'How glad I am to be home on my island again!'

From the naked roof of the barn, as I completed the repairs, I was uplifted by a kind of ecstasy with the vividness of the scene about me: the ever-changing tide-races, the brilliant colours of ocean and the distant white-margined rocks and cliffs, the whole horizon luminous under the galleons of the clouds, the radiance of the sun, and, as night fell, the rising of the clean stars.

The winter days were too short, flying past swiftly with this reconstruction work, so often interrupted by the need to prepare food, bake bread, wash clothes, collect driftwood (reserving the planks for repair work), and partner Jack in ferrying over the rabbit crop. When the weather was too wild to work on the roof I dug the bracken roots out of the little walled garden in front of the cottage, and repaired its tumbled-down hedge-walls so full of rabbit and bird holes. A robin was my close companion.

My one regret was the lack of time to begin immediately a study of the birds. But already I was overjoyed to find that the gales had not swept all of them from the island. Many had left, but with the harsher weather of midwinter other birds arrived, fleeing from the frozen mainland to the sanctuary of almost frost-free Skokholm.

O, the birds! Their flying forms, their wild mysterious beckoning cries!

Lying beyond any point of land, with no guiding cape or finger of mainland jutting towards it, Skokholm had few day-visitors. Chiefly the true migrants came, to stay a while, then pass on. But some flocks settled for the winter. How I welcomed them! For each bird was in a sense mine, a subject of my new kingdom, to be noted jealously, possessively, in my register of island birds each day, and listed with loving detail in the loose-leaf file of species recorded.

I recorded the flocks of redwings and fieldfares fleeing from cool Arctic lands; and the skylarks, pipits, starlings, wading birds, ducks and others which flocked from the mainland. Now and then there were rarities, such as the beautiful snow-buntings, so easily identified by their white-flashing wings; but others, with strange cries, flew past, exciting me, but I could not tell what they were.

This was my passionate joy, my principal sport – the possession of birds without hunting them to death, a personal frenzy to observe and record within this island of mine, this little kingdom of beauty ringed by the wide uncompromising ocean.

The small birds seemed to know quickly that I was harmless. Some came for shelter right into the cottage, through its numerous cracks – wrens, robins, dunnocks and blackbirds. Starlings slept in the chimney when the high tides and blinding sea-spray drove them from their normal night roost upon half the deck of a wrecked vessel which had long ago become jammed in the roof of Stack Cave. Some days more thousands of starlings arrived, a multitude of gossiping birds rolling in a magic carpet over the short turf as they dug their beaks into the soft ground in search of grubs.

The robin which lived in and out of the cottage had sung every day. Now, after the turn of the year, on a fine calm day, the resident blackbird began to tune his notes from his favourite perch on the broken roof of the cottage. When the sea was quiet then, I heard the skylarks begin their rich songs as the morning sun invited them to rise from their sleeping niches in the heathery fields. The gentle dunnocks, or hedge-sparrows, liked to creep about the garden, singing a brief shrill verse or two, flirting their wings alternately in those court-ship movements which have earned the bird the sobriquet of shufflewing. On the highest tufts of heather the resident pair of stonechats perched, handsome cock and sober hen, beady eyes alert for insects crawling on the ground.

The soft-voiced green-brown meadow pipits were always with me, strolling eagerly in the grass, sometimes in a flock, often singly. Many must have been northern breeding birds, come to winter in place of the island-breeding pipits, which had flown south. The cliffs and coast rocks were inhabited by the larger, darker rock pipits, each pair attached to its own stretch of territory. I could always be sure of a plaintive whistle of welcome from the pair which owned the landing steps when I returned from an expedition to the mainland.

Familiar sounds of the winter day were the melodious wailings of curlew and lapwing over the marsh in the centre of the island. Their music was loudest when the resident pair of ravens passed overhead. The lapwings mobbed the black pirates with darting flight and noisily zooming wings.

Crossing the long molinia grass of this moor, I would flush numerous long-billed birds from their delving in the winter-wet ground; handsome woodcock, zigzagging common snipe, and the straight-flighted little jack snipe. At night these birds boldly left cover to feed by every rill and damp corner.

The wild ducks which I had disturbed from the two main ponds returned from nowhere at dusk. Widgeon whistled home, and quacking mallard and teal dived through the sunset to wade and dabble and feed in the shallow water. The oystercatchers came up from the sea-rocks where they hunted shellfish all day, and added their piping notes to the wild chorus. In the morning, among the marks of a thousand webbed and unwebbed feet, I would find the broad imprints and grass-green droppings of wild geese, whose marvellous honking from chevron formations in the sky had stirred my soul at the going down of the sun, and at dawn.

The weird screams of the water rail – so like the cry of a wounded rabbit – skulking in the shelter of storm-battered bracken, would startle me. Sometimes I surprised the solemn face of a little owl, as this alien intruder sat framed in the doorway of a rabbit burrow, enjoying a ray of sunshine. On most days the ringing cry and butterfly-flight of the red-billed chough filled me with delight; for this handsome, harmless crow is rare today, haunting only the wildest parts of Wales, Ireland and the Hebrides. A pair were to linger into spring, to nest in a crevice in the sheer red walls of Mad Bay.

Lord and master of all the island birds, the magnificent peregrine falcon hunted starling, duck and wading bird, rising high for the deadly power stoop and striking each victim dead in mid-air with one blow of clenched talons. The little merlin came and stayed awhile, to chase the pipits and larks with tenacious twists and turns, until a frantic quarry miscalculated the last aerial trick. Now and then a migrating sparrowhawk flew in; its tactics were to beat swiftly and low over the ground, to flush some small bird, and sweep it up before it could gather its wings properly. The slow-moving kestrel hovered precisely on the sea-wind as if pinned to the sky; I saw it plummet upon mouse, beetle, worm or insect in the heather, then move to a fresh station in mid-air.

Buzzards were my daily companions, like lesser eagles soaring on broad pinions from one outcrop of rock to another. Leisurely in flight, majestic and dignified, they were cunning to seize any prey by surprise – a young crow foolishly absorbed in its daily bath, a frog or a slow-worm incautiously slipping through the grass, even worms in the dew. As vultures clear up carrion, my buzzards dealt with nature's casualties – the migratory bird battered by weather and too tired to move after crossing the sea, the sick rabbit, and the rabbit itself helplessly struggling in a snare.

Ranging the island cliffs, I would often see the sleek head of a grey seal rise from the white foam below. Although the coast is too sheer, and seldom free of a heavy ground swell, half a dozen of these fine beasts made the island waters their home. Their habit was to fish over the high tide. Many a time I watched how they dealt with giant conger and huge, wide-winged ray or skate. Bringing any larger fish they caught to the surface, they paralysed their victim with a few bites of those powerful jaws; then proceeded to play with it as a cat with a mouse, letting the fish swim feebly away, retrieving it and biting, and finally eating it – while the gulls hovering overhead snatched at the fishy crumbs floating on the water. As the sea ebbed on calm days the seals would clasp the rocks with flexible fore-flippers, and drag their quarter-ton weight ashore, to rest for a few hours in the sun.

At that time the fishermen of the coast shot them freely, but in later years, under total protection at Skokholm, they were to increase, and even occasionally to rear a calf in the rough boulders above the sand of North Haven.

*

Impatient for longer days in which to work and observe out of doors, I eagerly scanned earth and air for the first evidence of spring. The wind was still bitterly cold, there was even frost at intervals, but in the last of January the frogs spawned in the pond, the leaves of lords-and-ladies unrolled, and the first primrose appeared in the shelter of South Haven. On the second day of February Dick, the old rabbit-trapper, brought me the first shearwater I had seen alive since landing on the island last summer. I was very angry when I saw that both its legs were broken.

'Thought as thee'd like to see 'un,' said Dick, stroking the glossy back and white plumage gently. 'Aye, poor cocklolly!'

The old man had been a trapper all his life; yet he still had a thought for the suffering of a trapped bird. This and a certain dignity of carriage and address made you like Dick. He shared with me a passionate love of the island and its birds. He was altogether an unusual figure, and something of an ascetic. Money worried him little, and as for food, if he was trapping far from the house, at the other end of the island, he never troubled to come home for a meal midday. He preferred to tighten his belt and work on. When he returned at night he would sit close to the fire, poking it so that it never stopped blazing, and every now and then announcing some bird, ship, scene or incident of weather or work which came to his mind as he recalled the hours he had spent at his task that day. Often, his mind wandering, he re-told an incident which had happened days before.

But I was upset, and very tired of the slaughter of birds in the rabbit-traps. Fresh from my little farm in Monmouthshire, where rabbits were scarce and steel-jawed traps – to my knowledge – never used, how was I to know that these instruments took wholesale toll of wild birds? I was to discover from bitter experience that on an island as wind-swept as Skokholm birds used rabbit-holes freely in lieu of other shelter. Every bird that trod on the fresh earth (and many were naturally attracted to it) covering the trigger pan of a trap placed in the mouth of a rabbit burrow was doomed to broken legs and, since a bird with broken legs might as well be dead, a cruel death.

At first Dick, aware of my love of birds, had hidden from me the birds he had caught, but later I had wind of the slaughter. Returning one evening from the mainland, after a stormy crossing earlier that day, we surprised Dick roasting some blackbirds and thrushes over the driftwood fire. The old rascal had offered us a share. I determined that I would go round the traps with him next morning.

Too late I discovered that hundreds of all kinds of birds must have been caught that winter, judging by the number we picked up with the rabbits trapped that dawn. But it was hardly Dick's fault: I had taken the advice of Bulldog Edwards to make as much money as possible out of the rabbits with traps (but he had not mentioned birds being caught), money I so badly needed. I was to blame for not going around the traps with him earlier. My excuse was my pre-occupation with my self-appointed job of mason, cook, washerwoman and boatman.

Well, I would never use traps again. There would have to be some other method of taking the rabbit crop. I was not sure quite what, for we had tried ferrets, and they had been a failure – despite the fact that the island warreners of Norman times had used them almost exclusively. The success of those early ferreters may, I thought, have been due to the readiness of the rabbits newly introduced (from the mainland) to bolt from their traditional predators (ferrets, stoats, weasels); but after six or seven centuries continuously without these natural enemies below ground, and only man and gulls attacking them from above, the race of island rabbits had learned that their security lay in remaining below?

I intended to study how I might catch the rabbits in future without harming other wild life. Meanwhile, with the arrival of the shearwaters, trapping must stop.

I took the shearwater from Dick, saying: 'The cocklollies

have come home. That means we finish the rabbiting for the season. Pull up the traps, and I'll put you ashore, Dick, and you can dig your garden and set your early potatoes in good time.'

The beautiful little albatross struggled in my hands, its dark eye seeming to question my intentions. Hopeless to set its mangled legs in splints. I pulled its neck. I turned its warm body over and examined its long wings with their firm quills which make it such a perfect ocean glider. Short webbed feet placed so far to the rear of the body that it is unable to walk upright, and (as I had discovered last summer) it can only flop along with half-open wings supporting it. Evidently it was strictly nocturnal on land because of this helplessness which rendered it so vulnerable to attacks by the diurnal gulls? What sex was this individual? My bird guide book said the sexes in this species were indistinguishable in the field; but there were no precise details of its life history, either.

I must find out more about these mysterious shearwaters – if only I could spare the time from the task of getting a living. Meanwhile it was fascinating to speculate on why it had arrived so early. Probably, I thought, it was a mature male which, as in so many other species of birds, had arrived first to stake out a territory and advertise for a wife? And its first task would be to drive out the rabbits which had wintered in the burrow?

But I was wrong about the sex. I posted it to an expert ornithologist who had lately written to me asking for specimens to help him in his study of the moults of little-known birds. Harry Witherby replied:

Manx shearwater was interesting. Female. Ova well-formed, oviduct bulged in two places and undoubtedly a bird which had laid egg or eggs in its time – therefore adult! I mean, *not* a bird born last year. Nothing in stomach. Moult considerable on neck, throat and head . . .

The discerning editor of the monthly *British Birds* was quite excited by my specimen. His letter pleased me. I felt that the cocklolly had not been killed in vain. I was even more delighted when the thoughful Witherby next wrote:

The exact incubation period of the Manx shearwater is not known. It would be a good piece of work if you could observe this, and the exact fledging period. A record of a number of individuals would be safest and most valuable. Would ringing help you in this?

At that time Witherby was making and supplying numbered aluminium leg rings or bands by which individual birds could be identified. He sent me a few hundred: a kindness which was to revolutionize my method of study completely.

4 Spring

More and more shearwaters, glossy with good feeding, returned to the island in the next few weeks. Wandering at night over their burrows with a torch, I found them, singly at first, sitting tamely outside their holes, resting as if dazed, or perhaps merely happy to sleep a while on solid earth after the long winter of sea sailing. I handled each bird gently and firmly when banding it with a numbered ring, and I fancied that it accepted me, as I had accepted it, as a new and not dangerous companion (of course it would have no such anthropomorphic thoughts! The shearwater just happens by nature to be docile and slow in its reactions on land).

By good fortune a small colony of shearwaters was established in the shallow soil at the base of the rocky knoll immediately at the back of the house. Nothing could be more convenient for my purpose than to devote my limited time to banding and studying the individuals inhabiting the half a dozen burrows there. These were not deep, in fact the passages ran only a few inches below the turf, and with my arm and a small stick I could trace their windings to the recess at the end, where the bird and its partner would nest.

I carefully cut away the sod immediately above the recess in each burrow, tapering the cut so that I could fit the sod as a wedge to plug the hole, excluding the light but forming a convenient lid for inspecting the nest site. I promised myself that I would nevertheless disturb the inmates as little as possible, never more than one visit a day, preferably early in the morning, to give them time to settle back to sleep long before the activity of the night began. They might have time to regard the whole intrusion as part of a bad dream (if birds do dream).

As an observer I wished to efface myself, to avoid notice, to be as unobtruding as was consistent with the object of obtaining the scientific facts. Facts, always the facts. I must avoid sentiment.

Some weaknesses developed however. I rapidly acquired a fondness for my marked birds, and found myself giving them names in addition to their somewhat soulless band-numbers. At the entrance to each burrow I had placed an identification peg bearing a single letter. My system was to give each marked bird a name beginning with the index letter of its nest. Hence the pair in nest A became Adam and Ada; the pair in burrow B were dubbed Bill and Bess; the couple in C were registered as Carol and Caroline; and so on.

*

At this point I must digress for a moment to repeat once more that this book was intended to be the story of all the creatures of nature – mammal, bird, reptile, insect, flower – whose lives I was studying on the island. In short I had wished to paint a true picture of the ecology of this small sub-oceanic island. As a mere man I did not consider myself as directly part of that ecology. As an interloper, an accidental wanderer to the scene so to speak, I planned to leave my own life history out of it. But an expert naturalist who read the first draft chapters was indignant at the omission, claiming that as a man I was an essential ingredient – albeit somewhat predatory – influencing the island's ecology. He insisted that I should insert the main details of 'not necessarily your thoughts and emotions, but what you *did*, how your mode of living affected the lives of your creature islanders, what you killed and ate of them, what you protected, what you introduced, how you, too, built a home and nested (for I heard that you did). For at heart every man is a Crusoe and most of us will read your chapter on the ecology of the island man the most avidly of all in the book.'

It is true that I was in a sense nesting on the island. Perhaps I should explain that on leaving my Monmouthshire farm with the intention of becoming a voluntary Crusoe a curious and quite unexpected remark affected my whole future, so that I came to live on the island with the same expectation as the shearwater – of making a home for a partner. It came about in this way. When I said goodbye to a neighbouring small-holder with whom I had often worked and shared implements and tools (as was customary among local farmers) she had wished me success; but she had added suddenly, and with heartrending wistfulness, that she had always longed to pioneer on a small island. The despair in her eyes surprised me into the obvious courtesy of inviting her to join me – sometime next year, perhaps (I hastily added), when I should have restored the roof of the island cottage.

It was a curious contract, a solemn engagement, to be followed by a flow of letters: from me, island news which made her envious; from her, letters which spiced the solitude of that winter with the joys of anticipation. Let me admit that thoughts of the forthcoming marriage spurred me to greater efforts to prepare the nesting place for my mate.

Nevertheless I shall not burden the reader with the domestic details of the wedding which took place in the nearest seaside church in the following July, except to say that there was a roof on the cottage by then, a garden planted, and goats introduced for milking purposes. But as my new partner hoped, there was still much pioneering to be done, for which she had a noble appetite. She was quite able to take the place of a man in the boat, when Jack went ashore as usual that summer for the village hay harvest (I could little afford his wages at that time).

Nor need I record, except in passing, the birth of a daughter two years later, who was reared to school age entirely on the island. With her arrival the island idyll was complete. We were virtually self-supporting: enjoying the fruits of our labour in the garden, which produced simple vegetables and soft fruit in abundance (but no orchard trees would survive the gales); and goat's milk, butter and cheese, gulls' eggs, rabbits from the land, and fish and shellfish from the sea. Eventually we had a small flock of sheep, providing wool and meat. For firing there was always driftwood thrown up in some bay or creek, depending on the wind; and in winter this fiercely burning material could be checked, and our fire made to last the night through, by adding peat from the turbary on the marsh.

We needed to be self-supporting. It was a period of international depression. Prices for the surplus wool, lambs, rabbits and shellfish were extremely low. My slender capital had completely vanished in the initial purchases, and I might have been deep in debt at first had not yet another quite unexpected piece of luck come my way, even before I was married. Perhaps I ought to relate this incident, too, as it affected our economy so considerably.

It was late February, three weeks after the first shearwater had arrived, as already described. There had been a strong breeze from the east all night, accompanied by heavy mist. In the morning only a gentle zephyr was left. The sun rose upon a strange and tragic, yet beautiful scene as it bathed the island cliffs in clear light.

Quite incredibly – as it seemed to me – that old enemy of mine, rough weather, had quietly put ashore into a creek on the south-east point a wooden schooner in full sail! As if manoeuvred by an expert pilot, she lay broadside and upright against the red shore, her transom tight to the cliffs on the north wall, her bowsprit immovably wedged in low rocks on the south side of the gulley.

When you are as poor in worldly goods as I was, and you have lived long enough by the sea, everything that it gives up you are greedy to have. You may even dream of a great ship crushed on the shore, pouring out its life-blood of innumerable spars, machinery, cargo, tools and other treasure. It may be discreditable, but you could be less concerned about the loss of life – since you cannot revive a drowned man – than of the loss of the spoils of the wreck. I believe that some of my first thoughts when I saw the schooner were as disreputable as any confirmed beachcomber's.

Yet there was rapture, too, as in a beautiful dream. Oh, words can never explain the whirling thoughts in my brain at that moment! The wreck was so unbelievably theatrical, unreal, and, if I blinked my eyes, it would vanish? But first, were there any casualties?

There was nobody aboard when Jack and I scrambled down the cliffs and over the broken bowsprit to her deck. No soul alive or dead, unless you count her figurehead, which had been struck off by the rocks as she went ashore, and was now floating alongside, her bright painted face staring up into the blue sky – instead of down over the bow-wave. With a grapple we hauled her unceremoniously aboard, to save her from the greedy sea.

Alice Williams, topsail schooner, built 1854, had sailed superbly to her death, in the red walls of Skokholm. She had broken her keel on the huge, sharp boulders.

'She'll never sail the sea again,' Jack said, his eyes gleaming with the satisfaction of the true beachcomber he was. 'Better make the owners an offer and she yours!'

I went ashore and over the phone drove a bargain with the underwriters. At first they said they would tow the schooner away, after they had got over their surprise that she had not sunk. They told me that her captain and crew had abandoned her when, in the mist yesterday evening, she struck a rock near the entrance to Milford Haven. They had rowed to safety in the ship's boat, leaving the schooner apparently sinking and out of control. Reluctantly the underwriters agreed she was now useless to anyone except me. What was my offer?

In the end I bought *Alice Williams* for a nominal £5.

It is possible that her cargo of coal had somehow plugged the alleged leak. It is certain that she had sailed five miles through the mist of her own volition, with none to guide her, into the solid embrace of the island; and, for the needy islander, at the right moment – the top of the spring tide. She might now last a fortnight, over the neaps, before the next spring tide smashed her. Until then she was all mine!

I could hardly realize my extraordinary good fortune, for to me she was worth several hundred pounds in timber, furniture fittings and house-fuel; and what I might realize by selling her canvas and gear. But we must work like demons. I brought back with me to the island three volunteers willing to go 'wrecking'.

A rope from her deck-winch, reeved through the block of her topsail yard, which leaned conveniently inward over the sloping shelves of the creek, gave us the height and tackle for hoisting all the heavy stuff we could get out of the old ship – her splendid sails, her metal fittings, her deck houses, her spars. At high tide we rowed away the smaller items direct to the steps in South Haven in the *Storm-Petrel*. At low water, when the sea had ebbed from her hold, we hoisted the coal to the cliffs in baskets. We must have cached fifty tons or so, the big lumps built up as a retaining wall to hold the rest. A month later the razorbills were to find crevices in that black wall in which to hide their huge speckled egg.

When the spring tide turned, eighteen days after she had struck, an hour or two of strong onshore wind at high water tore the stripped skeleton of the once gracious schooner to shreds. The sea tossed her iron-hard oak timbers like match-sticks into the mouth of South Haven. We added these beams, baulks and planking to the mountain of material gathered, more than enough timber to re-roof and repair all the island buildings.

My helpers departed, each with some useful item of timber or gear from the wreck.

The barn was ready for us to move in. Jack and I fixed the schooner's brass-bound steering wheel in the breast of the chimney-piece we had built there to accomodate a new hearth. It was so contrived that, when turned, the wheel lifted or low-ered a chain on which kettle or stewpan might be hung over the fire. (Glittering with polish the handsome brass and mah-ogany wheel still dominates the interior of the old building, henceforth known as the Wheelhouse.) We transferred our living and sleeping gear.

By mid-March we were stripping and rebuilding the roof of the house. The schooner's oak timbers provided new beams – frame, collar and tie – to carry the purlins and rafters, which we cut from her pine deck planking. Her freshwater tank was fixed to catch the roof water. Her cabin steps became the stairs to the bedroom loft. Her galley and wheelhouse were rolled into position, intact, to serve as shelters for the milch goats and chickens. Her handrail was cut up and built in as framing to the hearth and fireplace in the living room. One of her top-masts was erected as a flag-pole on the rocky knoll behind the house.

As for her figurehead, *Alice Williams* was repainted and fixed immovably to the red rock above South Haven; and to this day she serves as an anchor mark to incoming boats.

5   Cocklollies

The galley of the schooner, placed in the farm fold, made a convenient shelter for a dozen Rhode Island hens which I had imported to provide fresh eggs until the gulls had laid theirs later in the spring. Although they had free range, with the conservatism of their ancestors the jungle fowl these hens never wandered far from our back door. They found that the dry earth thrown out of the burrows in spring-cleaning operations by my little colony of shearwaters made an ideal dust bath. On their part the shearwaters, conducting their love affairs at night, would pick up the moulted hen feathers and carry them below to line the nest.

It was not easy to observe their nocturnal activities; but by flashing a torch discreetly at brief intervals over the colony in the midnight hours I gradually pieced together the procedure of shearwater courtship without unduly disturbing them. But it was to take me ten years of banding and close study of individuals before the full life history of this charming little albatross was unravelled. Even so, much has remained a mystery, a challenge to continue the work.

Each evening, long before the sun dropped into the Atlantic Ocean, from March to August, many thousands of shearwaters gathered upon the sea between the islands of Skokholm and Skomer. On fine days it was pure delight for us to sail out to the rafts, trailing a line for mackerel and pollack. The shearwaters might be fishing, too, making their short dives after the whitebait which the mackerel were chasing: in the clear water you could see their wings were half-closed – a strong fan or paddle to winnow their way under the water. But most of the time the shearwaters floated, perfectly idle, perfectly silent, waiting for darkness, a marvellous magic carpet spread over quarter of a square mile of slow-swelling sea. The nearest flocks took wing languidly as the *Storm-Petrel* glided close: ten thousand pied bodies swerved low and tilted over, now white, now ebony in the rosy westward light.

The shearwaters were thickest on land during the blackest, stormiest, spring midnights, roaring home with wailing songs, and spending much time in scuffling outside the burrow, gossiping, disputing, settling their love affairs. Despite the bedlam there were differences in the individual calls. I became convinced that the birds recognized each other in the darkness by voice in the first place, and until they made contact physically. How else indeed could they (or for that matter we humans) know each other at a distance in the black void?

It was significant that on moonlit nights fewer shearwaters came home, and always without calling. Were they afraid of the island gulls, which could see and kill them on a bright night, when these predators sleep but lightly? On such nights the homing shearwater could see the burrows of its home colony clearly enough. It would fly silently straight to its hole and disappear immediately; once below it might give voice, in a connubial conversation with its mate, or in disputing territory with an intruder.

But I was puzzled by the fact that on dark nights the incoming screaming shearwater often got no response from its mate, either because it was not at home, or because when at home its mate did not always reply. Why scream at all? Was it solely from its desire to warn its mate of its arrival and get a welcoming voice in reply; was it just uninhibited *joie de vivre*; or was it also for some other reason?

It was a long time before I realized that one important explanation for the silence on a clear night, and the continuous screaming on dark nights, of the inflying bird approaching its nesting area, must be associated with the fact that the shearwater can no more see in the dark than we can. I came to believe that the shearwater uses a form of echo-location. Like the near-blind bat uttering its ultrasonic trill, or like the oilbird of Central America and edible-nest swiftlets of Malaysia which both give forth clicking notes in the utter darkness of their nesting caves, is the shearwater able to judge its distance from objects in the dark by receiving back from the contours of those objects (that is, the land) the echoes of its own screams, echoes whose specific audio-patterns it has learned from previous experience, and those patterns are now stored in its memory cells? First of all, perhaps, the loud cries of the incoming bird are reflected back from the main contours of the land, enabling the bird to judge by sound memory its nearness and so prevent collision. Then, circling nearer the home burrows, it picks up the familiar voice echoes of the nesting area, and at last plumps down on the turf.

Waiting beside my back-door colony on many a pitch-dark night, I was amazed at the accuracy with which each of my marked birds screamed its way to alight within a few feet of its burrow, which it could not see. Once on the ground the incoming bird invariably rested a minute or so. After the freedom of flying through the air at thirty to fifty miles an hour it needed to adjust to the solidity of the land in the darkness. I could imagine it thinking: 'Well, I'm somewhere near home. Let me see – my bump of location tells me to turn left here, then a little bit up hill by this old rabbit-track – then I'm home. I wish my mate below would sing out.' But whether there was a mate at home to guide it with invitatory cackles from below ground, or not, the new arrival would waddle solemnly to its burrow, feeling its way on foot with that strong sense of direction, or memory of geographical position, which most creatures seem to have.

*

To return to Adam and Ada, Bill and Bess, Carol and Caroline, and the others in the little shearwater 'village' of a dozen nests sited on the slopes of the knoll at my back-door. They all proved to be individuals with amusingly distinct voices, characters and idiosyncrasies; yet, like human beings, they conformed to the general biological pattern of behaviour specific to their kind. The partnership of Adam and Ada was typical. It proved to be without a blemish. They lived together inseparably for four years, until one of them died. 'Until death do us part' holds good for shearwater marriages.

What did you say? I hear my scientist readers growl. Yes, despite my determination to observe and record without sentiment and anthropomorphism, I found myself once more drawing comparisons between their habits and ours. It was no good – I could not help granting to them, even as I entered the scientific details of nest and band-numbers, date of egg-laying, incubation, and other habits, responses and reactions, etc., a measure of reasoning and individual action which alone makes life tolerable to the human spirit.

To me Adam and Ada, and the other marked individuals, had become very nearly human.

The marked pairs returned year after year to the same burrow. Usually the male was first home, late in February or early March. It seemed to me that this fact of lone arrival, and his behaviour in the next few days, cleaning up the burrow, and driving out the rabbits which had used it all winter, argued that he had lost touch with his mate over the long storms and wandering at sea over the winter. One never saw pairs of shearwaters at sea in any season; only singletons, or flocks. Besides, at the end of the breeding season, each bird would begin moulting, always a difficult period in the yearly cycle.

Be that as it may, Adam each year seemed to be preparing the nest-site in excellent time for Ada, like an eager experienced male determined to hold his territory. It was obvious from the very first season of observation that he was an old adult. You had only to look at his feet. There were holes and splits in the webs, his claws were blunt, and some missing; in fact the first half-inch of the toes of his right foot had been nipped right off at some time – a clean bite as if a fish had attacked but failed to hold him.

Yes, it was my older adults which staked their claim in the village earliest each spring. Ada – also fully mature – would arrive a few days, perhaps a week, later than Adam. Then began a familiar courtship all over again. What conversations went on below the turf! From the throaty chuckles, and occasional full screams, it sounded as if they were going over the details of their winter adventures. One thing seemed certain: as in all birds it was necessary for the shearwaters to re-establish the pair-bond after each winter of separation. This required elaborate ceremonies, if only to break down the habit of keeping at a safe distance from other birds by which the individual survives danger of sudden attack in the non-breeding season.

It fascinated me to think that Adam and Ada had never had a good look at each other in a clear light. These ceremonies took place in the dark, either outside the burrow on dark nights, or inside it when the moon was bright. They would never know how beautiful they were, to me or to each other.

'Nice to be home! (you could fancy Ada saying). Hullo Adam! Your voice hasn't changed a bit. I could do with a long sleep. No horse-play please, not yet. Keep your distance.' And Adam would have to confine his ardour within the bounds of a delicate nibbling of her face and bill with his beak, or risk a severe rebuff.

There was no actual mating for several weeks, but the pair drew closer together in their courtship play, in lining the nest and guarding it. They took turns to stay over the day. Occasionally both were present by day; but sometimes over moonlit periods both might be absent. Yet it was dangerous to leave the burrow untenanted: possession is nine-tenths of the law, and seems to give the occupant extra might to enforce the moral right. In the absence of the rightful owner other shearwaters looking for a home or partner might enter a prepared burrow; in the pre-egg stage this often happened, although these intruders did not necessarily stay over the following day. Then, when powerful old birds like Adam or Ada returned there would be a fight with the interloper, and screaming. ('I found it empty! My back's to the wall!' 'Yes, but I dug and cleaned it out long ago! Its mine! I only slipped off to get a square meal last night! Clear out!' 'Shan't!' 'No? Then I'll drag you out!')

The hullaballoo in the total darkness would usually end with the tough experienced old one forcibly ejecting the weaker, nervous and generally unpaired younger bird. But if, as also happened occasionally in seasons of overcrowding, two established pairs were competing for the same burrow, ultimate possession might go to either, depending perhaps which female laid the egg first and started incubation. (Unless I caught the birds in the act of copulation, or unless I found the female on the new-laid egg, I could not at first tell the sex of the shearwater, so alike are the pair to the human eye. Both develop the same sized brood patch, free of feathers, below the breast, into which the egg fits warmly against the naked skin. Later I learned how to sex sea-birds from an examination of the cloaca.)

I was puzzled by the irregularity of the shifts of nest-guarding. Sometimes the male remained several days, and therefore the intervening nights too, at home, and sometimes it was Herself did duty. This haphazard rota was continued even after mating took place.

The honeymoon period between the marriage and the laying of the single large white egg lasted for about three weeks. Then, for several nights before the egg appeared, the female disappeared, leaving her mate to guard the prepared nursery. It was almost as if, having mated, she was avoiding him now. She returned just before, or on the day of, laying the egg. On the next night, if her mate was present, she handed the egg over to him and departed.

This was the general but not invariable pattern. The female, exhausted after egg-laying, spent several days and nights away at sea. Her husband sat phlegmatically brooding the egg all day, bill tucked into his feathers. When I lifted the sod over the recess he would raise his head sleepily, confused by the light. A quick check on his band number, and I would slip him back in place. I hoped he might regard the whole swift interruption as part of a bad dream?

The incoming bird never brought food to feed its mate at night, whether or not the guard was changed. Although each loses quite a lot of weight during long shifts at the nest, their life-history was to prove to me that they can withstand long fasts. Some of the shifts on the egg lasted as much as ten days, but the average was about five. Five days of twenty-four hours meant 120 hours of continuous fasting. But the bird on duty in the burrow was warm and dry, and wasted little energy in movement; at most it turned itself and the egg round at intervals, and now and then scratched at the fleas and lice which troubled it.

This arrangement of shifts of several days was extremely interesting, and something quite unrecorded in the literature of incubation. In other species one partner fed the other if it stayed many days on the nest. It was clear that the shearwater pair took fairly equal shares: one was to fast at home while the other feasted at sea, for so many days at a time. 'Adam,' said Ada, 'I am off for a week-end at sea.' 'Very well my dear,' replied Adam, 'Will it be a long or a short week-end?' 'Aha!' said Ada mysteriously, 'that all depends on the little fishes. Au revoir!'

The only information on incubation I could find in the text books stated that the period was 'about one month'. But as in that first summer of observation not a single egg in the knoll village had hatched on the fortieth day of incubation, I began to be apprehensive that my peering into the burrows and daily handling of bird and egg was causing the eggs to become addled. Certainly by this date – early June – the egg in each burrow looked lifeless; it was no longer white, but smeared and brown with dirt.

On the forty-second morning I found Adam and Ada together in the recess, apparently in consultation over the unhatched egg. What had gone wrong? They could not know – as I hastily covered them up again – that I was just as worried as they might be.

On the fiftieth day the egg eclipsed all records for incubation that I knew of. The stork takes thirty days, the osprey thirty-five, the swan thirty-eight, the eagle forty and the vulture forty-eight.

On the fifty-first day I decided I would test Ada's egg for hatchability by candling it as one candles a hen's egg. I would shake it gently to detect its rotten contents washing to and fro (yet so far I had not detected any unpleasant odour in the burrow, which incidentally the mated pair always kept very clean).

But to my delight the egg had pipped, and the chick called faintly from within. I pushed it back under Ada's snow-white tummy. She uttered a little half-strangled cry of protest and stabbed at my hand. I fancied she looked positively maternal. I gave her an adoring look, thanked her aloud, and shut her into darkness again.

Next day the chick had emerged from the shell, a dark ball which soon dried out beneath Ada into a charming tiny downy object, helplessly weak for the first few days. Fifty-two days to hatch! But this was to prove the normal incubation period for the Manx Shearwater.

Turn and turn about Adam and Ada shared the job of brooding their child during the first week. It was defenceless enough to require their protection. But once its splendid blue-grey down was fluffed out it needed little warmth, and by day it sat beside, rather than beneath, its parent.

The parent away at sea returned with a load of food, but the process of feeding the chick was difficult to follow. In the cliff-burrows the puffins had long hatched their sturdy black chicks, and all day were carrying sprats, sand-eels, and small fry to feed them. You could see exactly what was being delivered, for Mr and Mrs Puffin like to stand about, as if proud of the bill full of little fishes, for several minutes, before diving into the burrow to hand them over, raw and straight from the sea. The feeble shearwater chick however could not cope with raw fish. Adam and Ada swallowed everything they caught at sea. In their dilatable stomachs the fish was partly digested, the gizzard arresting and grinding up hard bones. The stomach juices softened the food to a semi-fluid pulp. In this state it was regurgitated and fed to the chick.

By opening the nest at night as soon as complacent faint hunger cries and gurgling noises from below indicated feeding in progress, I pieced together the process. The chick would become excited on the arrival of the adult in the entrance passage. Calling and pecking towards the source of food in the darkness it was directed no doubt by the powerful smell of fish soup in the throat of the parent. While the chick was very small the parent would bend down and scoop up the tiny bill, and hold it tenderly in its own. Both adult and chick now vibrated the throat in pumping motions which assisted the flow of the semi-liquid pulp into the baby gullet. The parent deliberately controlled this flow, by constricting the muscular entrance to its oesophagus: the food trickled out in proportion to the ability of the chick to swallow it.

But as the chick grew strong it would eagerly fence with its bill to find the parental mouth in the darkness, and, thrusting its beak cross-wise within the opened mouth of the adult, would suck down ever larger dollops of the warm semi-digested fish food. By the time it had grown its first feathers, about the 40th day, the chick was capable of absorbing – when both parents fed it on the same night – very nearly half its own body weight of food in a single hour!

Alone by day after the first week, Hoofti (as for some unaccountable reason we dubbed the first chick of Adam and Ada) responded to our intrusion with a pattern of behaviour which was to prove typical of all shearwater chicks. It stabbed at the approach of our hand, of a rabbit, even of its own parents. It stabbed at everything – an instinctive but most useful reaction when you consider it, for such a movement both intimidated its enemies by day and brought its bill into delicious contact with those of its parents by night. 'Good old Hoofti,' I said to him (or her), as each day I studied the growth and development of Number One chick in the village.

On 1 August, the thirty-fifth day of his life, Hoofti was covered in down nearly two inches long – the first natal down was still attached to a second growth. He had vanished beneath this astonishing screen – an enormous rich grey-blue powder puff. To find his head I had to steer my hand around the ball until it was attacked by the sharp hooked bill shooting forth from cover; his eye had somehow seen my hand, although I could not see his eye without parting the down hanging over it.

Days passed into weeks, into two months. What was Hoofti doing and thinking alone by day for so long, growing so slowly? Over some bright nights neither parent visited him. On good dark nights one or both invariably came. After feeding him, they might stay a while, conversing with little screams and squabbling noises. They might even pluck from the turf and carry below some dwarf flowers and sorrel leaves. I would like to be able to believe that they brought these decorations to amuse Hoofti; but that would be too anthropomorphic altogether. First of all, Hoofti could not see such toys (remember, he had never seen his parents except perhaps in the faintest of light filtering into the burrow at night). Secondly, in spare moments, Adam and Ada were fond of plucking at objects near the burrow entrance. The student of animal behaviour calls all such inconsequential action 'displacement activity'; but the term aptly applies equally to the play of human child and adult. Lastly, I found that shearwaters eat a certain amount of this greenstuff – especially the astringent leaves of sheep's sorrel – evidently as a cat or dog does, perhaps idly but also because they enjoy it, and without knowledge that it supplies a tonic to the system.

No, it was not possible to know what Hoofti was thinking about. He was very much alive, ready to defend himself, but he did not like my daily intrusion. He would shuffle away into the darkness of the passage if I left his roof open for a while. He had seen nothing of the pageant of wild flowers which was visible from the knoll slope, the purple acres of the bluebells, the bright pink of the thrift, and the beautiful spikes of the foxgloves along the hedge-walls. Now in August the heather was in flower; and outside his very doorway the honey-coloured honey-filled bells of the wood-sage nodded plenti-fully in the sea-wind.

Very likely, if ever he saw these flowers in after years, Hoofti might not register the picture except in black and white; for he would always see them by night. Probably shearwaters are colour-blind: of what use is bright colour to black and white birds which live in the darkness while on land, catch their food under water, and by day roam white distances over dark seas?

On the sixtieth day of his life Hoofti was completely feath-ered, with only a ruff of down picturesquely about his neck, thighs and tail. He was very fat, heavier in fact than his parents. He wore a handsome new suit of black and white, identical with theirs except that their adult feathers had become ragged and soiled with the hard work of the nesting season. The ap-proaching moult would however provide them with a new winter suit as good as Hoofti's.

And by the way, where were Adam and Ada? I had not seen them often in the latter part of August. There was a cob-web in the entrance to their burrow on the morning of 27 August, the sixty-first day of Hoofti's life. And inside the burrow the rampart of the nest-lining and moulted down which surrounded the fat child was unbroken.

That night I waited for Adam and Ada to appear. It was good blustery shearwater weather, with dark showers and hardly a star to be seen. Here and there some adults came in after midnight, and visited other burrows, but not Adam or

Ada. Getting cold, I slipped a small sod in the entrance to Burrow A.

I wandered over the island, examining some of the great colonies of shearwaters at the west end. And there I made two surprising discoveries. I found several young birds at about the same stage as Hoofti, feathered but with much down still clinging, each *outside* the entrance to its burrow. I thought they must be on the way to the sea. Some lifted their wings as if to fly; but instead flapped them for several seconds, then were motionless again. My torch showed that some were preening, rubbing the beak and the back of the head in the oil gland at the base of the tail, and applying the exudation to the rest of the body – thus by an instinctive response (to itchiness) usefully waterproofing their new feathers. And always the wing-flapping.

Presently one by one, before the eastern sky grew light, they slipped below ground. I realized that the wing-flapping and preening was but a preliminary preparation for life at sea. These downy youngsters were not yet ready. But in order to exercise their long wings they had to come outside; there was no room below.

It was now very calm. A few adults were hurrying from the burrows towards the sea, but lack of wind prevented them becoming air borne. They blundered cliffwards. A few made straight for a steep ridge of outcropping rock. Using their beak, wings and claws they hooked themselves up the almost vertical surface, expertly, as to the manner born. One by one, reaching the top, they launched with a leap into the air, and glided safely clear. Another discovery for me – but I could only admire their good sense.

Examining the outcrop with my torch I saw a regular groove worn in the rock, evidently made by generations of shearwaters during immemorial summers they had nested here. So, when they needed a high take-off point in calm weather, they simply used this venue of the local gliding club!

Back at the knoll village, I saw that the sod in the entrance to Hoofti's burrow had not been touched. He had not been visited by his parents. I left the sod in place.

It remained unmoved for six days, proving that Hoofti remained indoors, unvisited and fasting, for some 144 hours.

Then on the morning of 3 September the sod had been pushed right out – but not by Adam or Ada – by Hoofti himself. There was plenty of his moulting down attached to the sod to prove that he had at last, like the youngsters at the west end, plucked up the courage to look at the outer world. He had tasted freedom and the wind on his face for the first time, exercised his wings, then gone back in.

On the next evening I watched beside Burrow A. The nights were longer now. Hoofti appeared, shoving the sod before him, just one hour before midnight. He did not seem to notice me, and I did not disturb him except to flash my torch when he moved. He flapped his wings, rested a while, flapped and preened at intervals for nearly two hours, before retiring to the burrow once more.

He was now above nine weeks old. He had broken every fledging period for a British bird that I had read of. But he did not prove an exception – every young shearwater that I studied subsequently, both in the knoll village and elsewhere, conformed to this pattern – not hitherto recorded in the bird books. The parents, worn down with the long weeks of care for the plump baby, gave up feeding altogether when it was at its fattest and heaviest, about the sixtieth day. Too gross and tender of feather to proceed to the sea, the abandoned chick remained fasting and unmoving in the burrow for six more days, during which it shed much of the down and completed the growing of its quills and body feathers. It lost weight steadily.

Around the sixty-sixth day it emerged, at night only, and for six more nights it adopted the same procedure of some two hours of exercise and preening and oiling its feathers before retiring. Then, much thinner and more agile, it flopped and scrambled its way to the sea. On a night of very strong winds it might even, I observed, be airborne almost from the nest, and fly steadily to the sea. But usually these untrained youngsters, totally unguided by any parent or other bird, virtually blundered along, taking the easy way downhill, and, since all slopes lead to the sea, eventually tumbled into the water. Total fledging-period – seventy-two days!

It is easy to imagine that the abandoned young shearwater is finally driven out of its burrow by hunger and thirst. But it is dangerous to credit a bird of such tender age, and no experience of gathering its own food, with conscious thought or awareness and knowledge of hunger or thirst. One might as well believe that the butterfly which lays her eggs on the foodplant of its species does so because she is aware that the eggs will hatch into caterpillars next summer and develop in her own image. We are told by the ethologist that the young shearwater, and the egg-laying butterfly, act quite by instinct, by no process of conscious thought, but following a behaviour pattern which they have inherited in their genetical make-up. We must believe that the mechanism controlling these set rhythms in the life cycle are to be found somewhere in the chromosomes and genes packed into the fertile egg, if only the bio-chemist can locate and separate the working parts of such a delicate and complicated living engine.

There is no escape from this unproven hope of the modern research biologist; unless you leave it all to God the Creator?

We must leave this province of the laboratory and theology to resume our study in the field. Many young shearwaters fail to reach the sea at their first attempt. They may get held up in dense bracken, perhaps far in the centre of the island. In the dawn most of these will be attacked and killed by gulls if they fail to hide in some hole or other cover. On many mornings in September I would go forth with a basket, to try to anticipate the murderous gulls, and bring back a load of these helpless lost youngsters. I would throw them one by one into the sea in South Haven. There they were safe. They would swim expertly, vigorously, away from the land. If a gull swooped at them, they would dive deep, and swim far under the water, coming up a long distance away. Until they became strong on the wing the sea was their element, safer than the air.

On our crossings to and from the mainland on these September mornings we would see some of the night's exodus of young shearwaters swimming with perfect ease, but always alone. They paddled towards the open sea, and had all vanished by mid-morning.

Where were they going? They could not be following the adults, at least not visually, for the old birds had departed half a month earlier. Only extensive banding of these shearwaters would answer that question. According to the experts thousands would have to be banded to get adequate results, the average recovery rate for all birds banded being extremely low, often under one per cent for some species.

There is no space here to do justice to all the characters which lived in the shearwater village on the knoll over the eleven years before the Second World War interrupted my studies. But I must mention briefly the affairs of certain principal individuals, as shown in the Table of Marriages, to whom I became specially attached because of their long association and

Table of Marriages of some Leading Shearwater Characters

YEAR	NEST A	NEST B	NEST C
1929	Adam and Ada	Bill and Bess	Caroline and Carol
1930	,,	,,	,,
1931	,,	(did not return)	,,
1932	,,		,,
1933	(Ada did not return)	Adam and Baby	,,
1934	Baby and R T 9346	Adam and Caroline	
			NEST CE
1935	,,	(Adam did not return)	Caroline and Carol II
1936	(Baby died in homing experiment)	Carol II and R W9948	Caroline and Carol III
1937	R S2317 (Venice homing experiment) and mate	,,	,,
1938	,,	,,	Caroline and Carol IV
1939	,,	,,	,,

faithfulness. It was my joy to spend a little time with them daily, to have some gossip, perhaps some scandalmongering, with my nocturnal neighbours, and so to gather yet more information on their surprising, fascinating lives. Also I must admit my natural laziness usually made me disinclined, after a busy day earning my bread fishing, shepherding and gardening, to go farther afield than the knoll outside my door.

If I had had more time I ought to have started earlier on an extensive banding campaign outside the colony. For the whole island had become a vast metropolis of shearwaters. My original estimate of 10,000 pairs had had to be doubled in a few years. The shearwaters on Skokholm have been increasing ever since the virtual cessation of ploughing in the last century when the Harrisons left (page 175); and they continued to spread after Bulldog Edwards departed, and the present total protection began with my arrival. The increase is plain in the extended burrowing underground right across former arable fields. Today there may be 35,000 pairs breeding, judging by the results of banding some 100,000 shearwaters at Skokholm, including thousands of young birds from which (through knowledge of the annual mortality) it has been possible to calculate the population of adults.

*

Even in those early years when I was studying the occupants of my backdoor village, there was some interference by rabbits and puffins. But above all there were moments of over-crowding caused by the shearwaters themselves. Unbanded individuals gate-crashed in established burrows, and were mostly ejected by the 'lawful' banded owners, or more rarely won the fight and stayed. Not infrequently random digging of new burrows by home-seeking colonists penetrated my marked burrows. To maintain some order and encourage my cherished pairs in possession, I might have to restore the situation, by blocking with earth and stone these advances, which from experience I knew could end in fighting and confusion in which egg or tender chick could be lost. An earlier attempt to map out a few square yards of the complicated burrow system at the west end of the island, where shearwater, puffin and rabbit competed in a dense and deep-dug underground slum, had shown me how impossible it was to keep track of individuals in these interlocking runways and recesses.

With occasional help from me therefore, Adam and Ada maintained possession of the desirable Burrow A for four happy years. Next door, in B, Bill and Bess had some difficulty with other shearwaters and burrowing rabbits; and they disappeared after the second year.

When Ada did not return in the fifth year Adam eventually found a new young-looking mate (Baby). It was a spring-time of over-crowding in the village, with much digging in every direction. I banded more than forty adults competing for homes. Eventually fifteen pairs struggled to pack into only twelve suitable nest recesses! Nest A deteriorated so much that Adam and Baby moved into Nest B; but the partnership was not a success. Her egg failed to hatch. And in the next spring, Baby, arriving very late, moved back into A, attracted thereto by a mate with a new band (R T9346).

This did not worry me, because in that (sixth) year the impatient Adam, settled permanently now in B, had already found a new wife in my favourite bird, the lady Caroline, who had been the original female in Nest C.

It can be seen from the Table of Marriages that Caroline was attached all her observed life to Nest C, except in that one year when, having lost her first husband Carol, she moved over to join her contemporary Adam in Nest B. Jilted (if I may use the word) by his young wife of yesteryear (but, as I have said, Baby returned very late – in fact, long after Adam had started to court Caroline), Adam seemed happy with a steady lady of his own age. Of course it was not the first time he had met Caroline. My records showed that on odd dates in previous years they had met together for a day in the same shelter, in the early spring – the 'visiting time' for older shearwaters. So I did not at first attach much significance to finding them together in mid-April of that sixth year. They would soon be separated and living with their mates of last year.

Adam and Caroline however settled down to long conversations in Nest B. Over the period of the April new moon they were there each night, busy lining the recess with the bulbs and pale-green underground swords of the bluebells, with grass and odds and ends. It looked as if, after all, they were going to make a go of it, as the saying is. The freshness of early love might not be theirs, or so I fancied. Probably they were an old, life-toughened pair, but with the spring even an old stager's thoughts may turn to . . .

Adam mated with Caroline. I caught them in the act when I opened the nest one night late in April. They were a tame, a delightful, pair. Long may they live together, I prayed.

My prayer was in vain. But at least they spent one happy summer together. It proved an ideal marriage, and all went well with the egg and the chick. In due course this nestling was given a numbered ring, but he became to us simply Hoofti V, because he was Adam's fifth child.

Hoofti V distinguished himself in an unusual way. Some papers I had written on the incubation and fledging of the shearwaters had appeared in a scientific journal, and attracted the interest of ornithologists. As this year happened to be the year of the Eighth International Ornithological Congress meeting at Oxford, my friend H. F. Witherby had asked us to receive on the island the members of the congress. As a gesture of international goodwill they would be conveyed to Skokholm in two of HM destroyers seconded from the Royal Navy. Among the sea-birds of the island they would be most anxious to see would be the shearwaters. I therefore roped the knoll colony around to prevent over-eager visitors trampling the flimsy burrows.

8 July 1934 turned out a beautiful day. Two hundred people of many nations signed their names at the door of our humble cottage before they marched past the knoll, where Hoofti V, in his long dress of blue-grey down, was lifted up to their gaze. If only, I thought, Hoofti could have seen them with my inward eye he would have said to himself, as I did: 'A strange crowd! But look, how wonderfully happy they are to see Hoofti V on this lovely summer day – why, a mere bird can smash petty nationalism, and all the world unite in homage to a fragile morsel of life, a nestling bird!'

But Hoofti was sleepy. He took no notice of the smiling greetings in Dutch, French, Spanish, German, Norwegian, Hungarian, Bulgarian, Latvian and English of many overseas kinds, and so many other tongues, paying tribute to the ball of fluff in my hand. He complained a little to me in his squeaky treble voice, disliking the bright sunlight, impatient to be returned to the peace and darkness of Nest B.

Then came a command performance. That ardent bird-lover, the ex-king Ferdinand of Bulgaria, had suppressed the fierce daggers of his gout and tottered as far as the top of the knoll, where his aide-de-camp had placed him in his portable armchair. There, while the other members of the congress roamed the island for an hour looking at the sea-birds, he rested in the cool northerly zephyr and watched the gulls, oystercatchers, puffins and wild flowers at all points of the compass about him. But walk a step farther this old man dared not. I carried Hoofti V to his hand.

'*Puffinus anglorum!* The young bird of *Puffinus anglorum!* Wonderful, wonderful! Yes, it is beautiful!' The long fingers of this German prince, this deposed king of the Bulgars, those fingers which had signed letters of state and treaties and – in his own notorious words – other 'scraps of paper', stroked the fine down of the child of Adam and Caroline admiringly.

'And where will this young bird fly when it leaves the burrow?'

'I'm afraid I don't yet know. But I am trying to find out by banding as many as possible.'

For a while Ferdinand (who was known to be a sound ornithologist even if he had failed as a king) talked to me of birds in his excellent English. He expressed his wonder at the strange life my wife and I and four-year-old daughter lived on this little kingdom in the sea. He even sounded a little envious.

'Yes, truly it is beautiful here. You are a wise young man. How peaceful it is! And all these thousands of birds, above and below ground! Yes, I shall never forget this day!'

He had signed his name on our roll as 'The Count of Murany'; but in his letter of thanks a few days later he enclosed his portrait with the bold signature: *Ferdinand Rex.*

6   Mystery of Migration

Were we really living such a strange life? Six years of island existence had only taught me how little I knew about the creatures I had intended to study. So much time had vanished in the mere occupation of getting our bread and butter. But to have done everything with our own hands was some satisfaction. Island life was vivid, and although we were poor in worldly wealth, we were extremely healthy, and physically as hard as nails. I daresay the curious, admiring members of the International Ornithological Congress may have thought in their hearts that our little house and the old buildings on the island were in a sorry state yet. But they should have seen Skokholm when I first found it.

Those early years were the best, despite the hard work. With Ann too young for school, the summers were idylls of fishing, sailing and sun-basking, when the body acquired a tan to last through the winter. Jack was no longer with us. We lived alone on garden produce, fish, rabbits, gulls' eggs, honey, and the milk, butter, cheese and meat provided by our goats and sheep. We shared the daily tasks of the house and garden, collecting gulls' eggs and driftwood, digging peat, watching and banding birds, listing flowers, and sailing across to the mainland for letters and simple groceries.

As long as the coal from the *Alice Williams* had lasted we could laugh at winter gales. While the little house shuddered in the cool Atlantic hurricanes, all was aglow within doors, where the hearth supported a bonfire of the fiercely burning gas coal with a log of driftwood atop spurting blue salt-flame. (But now the supply was running out, and we needed to gather and dry more peat each summer, to supplement the driftwood.)

In the evenings, inside the fortress of the island cottage, whose roof I had so lovingly made water- and wind-tight with each slate bedded in mortar above the timbers from the wrecked schooner, while the winter gales howled around, the hours passed swiftly as I wrote down observations on birds, flowers, weather and our daily experiences. And on the fine calm days the time flashed by in tasks outdoors, and the occasional visit to the mainland.

We were no longer dependent on the rabbit crop. Although I caught many each winter for the pot, and during the summer, I would not use again the cruel gin-traps. The rabbits, multiplying each year, were slowly gaining the ascendancy over the grazing. But my small flock of sheep and the goats, eating much of the coarser herbage disliked by the rabbits, were as yet thriving and profitable. Gradually, too, I ceased to fish for lobsters, crayfish and crabs for a summer living; maintaining only a few lobster-pots to supply our table. The lobstering had been exciting at first, but it had never been so profitable as the fishermen had boasted. And I had lately discovered to my surprise that I could earn more money, or at least enough for our simple needs, by writing articles commissioned by editors of national papers. These had come as a result of fresh observations on birds which I had published in scientific journals.

This opportunity was not without its embarrassments as well as its advantages. While we shunned the advances of the popular press and radio, who for a while had 'discovered' the Crusoe family Lockley, and endeavoured in vain to exploit us as curiosities, the publicity brought many genuine friends among naturalists. We were glad to have them to stay with us in summer, and help with the banding of the island birds.

Even before the International Congress visited us, these good friends had assisted in my plan to band every bird we could lay hands on, including the migrants which passed through Skokholm, often in large numbers, in spring and autumn. And I had been to Heligoland in the North Sea to study the traditional method of the islanders there of catching birds (for food) in large funnel-traps made of netting.

In 1933 we built the first migratory bird marking station – a

Heligoland-type trap in the garden. After that it was for us to organize the succession of visiting amateur bird-watchers so that as far as possible observational and banding work was continuous. More traps were built. Thousands of sea-birds were now being ringed each summer.

Luckily the island was too inaccessible to be troubled with sight-seeing day-visitors. Those whom we invited to stay discovered that they had to share in the daily chores of caring for the house and garden, gathering and milking the goats, collecting driftwood, carrying water. For us it was a joy and a revelation to have these genuine island- and bird-lovers helping us so intelligently, and the co-operative study was to result in many interesting new facts emerging.

Skokholm became the first Bird Observatory in the British Isles.

There is never an end to knowledge. The more I learned about the shearwaters, the less I seemed to know. I wished I had been able to answer ex-king Ferdinand's question: where did young Hoofti go in the winter time? He had remained for two weeks after Adam and Caroline had abandoned Nest B. I never saw him again, to recognize him. Nor did I see Adam again. But Caroline remained in the village, and she was the oldest inhabitant when observations closed down for the duration of the war.

How does a sea-bird find its way over the apparently trackless ocean? In her eighth year of residence Caroline was the subject of the first homing test we made, in an endeavour to discover this. Some interesting experimental work had been done in the past. Lashley and Watson in America had had some success with noddy and sooty terns returning from distances outside the known geographical range of these species. Rivière, working with homing pigeons in England, had reached the conclusion that these domesticated doves had a distinct 'sense of geographical position'. In 1935 I had myself conducted an experiment with the help of the editor of the *Racing Pigeon*, Major W. H. Osman, who had sent me five young untrained pigeons from lofts in London. I released them on the mainland opposite Skokholm, 240 miles from London. The object was to discover if absolutely untrained young pigeons could return over such a formidable distance.

An east wind with slight haze, such as prevailed at the moment of release, has often proved too much for trained birds, and is reckoned to be the worst homing weather for pigeons. None of them returned. But I was not very surprised. The homing pigeon is descended from the rock-dove, a non-migratory species.

David Lack, biology master at Dartington Hall School, camping at Skokholm in June 1936 with the bird-watching children of Bertrand Russell, Stephen Leacock and Clough Williams-Ellis, took back with him to Devon Caroline and two other shearwaters each wearing a numbered leg band. Two days later, at 14.00 hours, he released Caroline from the far south-east point of Devon, the lighthouse at Start Point, which is 225 miles from Skokholm by the sea-route around the Land's End of Cornwall.

David sent me a letter recording how Caroline had flown straight out to sea, that is, southwards: but that letter did not reach me until *after* Caroline returned! Meanwhile I watched each night from the day of David's departure.

Caroline came home, the first shearwater to arrive that evening, in 9¾ hours after release at Start Point. A remarkable performance, for it argued that she had instantly recognized where she was, after two days solitary confinement in a box during the long train and road journey, and that she had made straight for Skokholm, presumably by the sea-route. 225 miles in under ten hours means an average surface speed of about 25 m.p.h., but in fact a shearwater does not fly straight but has a side-to-side deviating flight. In effect this would require Caroline to fly much faster than 25 m.p.h. to get home to her nest in that short period of ten hours; and therefore she could have had no time to find her way to Skokholm by random searching.

Caroline *knew* where she was. But how? I pictured how helpless I would have been under similar circumstances: transported in a closed box, by boat, car, train, car and then (supposing I had wings but no navigational instruments or map), thrown over a cliff into the English Channel. Could I have found Skokholm in just under ten hours? Could I have found Skokholm at all? Of course, Caroline probably knew the English Channel well, since it is within the normal range

of this shearwater. But pehaps she had flown direct in the end
– 126 miles overland?

Unfortunately the long journey in the boxes had been too
much for the other two shearwaters, and they had died by the
time Start Point had been reached. A week later I myself was
off on a visit to the Faeroe Islands, and thought it would be a
good plan to take with me a shearwater or two and try an
experimental release much farther from home waters. But I
would not risk my precious Caroline again. Instead I took the
widow (thinking she could not rear a chick alone) of one of the
two which had died on the way to Devon and another female
of six summers' breeding. I carefully packed each in a box and
guarded them all the way by train and ship for three days until
the Danish vessel *Primula* was one hundred miles south of the
Faeroe Islands, on her way to Iceland and 610 miles away from
Skokholm. Then in fine weather I released one bird.

She swept grandly away to the south. Marking her direction
on the ship's chart, I saw that she was heading for Skokholm –
surely a remarkable coincidence? But Ekholdt, the captain of
the *Primula*, who had taken such a keen interest in the birds,
looked at me in awe, saying: 'Wonderful! That, I think, is what
you call instinct?'

I said nothing. At that stage I disliked the word 'instinct'.
But, as we shall see, Ekholdt was quite right.

Next morning as we entered the mist-wreathed Faeroe
Islands, I released the other shearwater, 730 miles from home.
She vanished at once in the foggy distance.

One of the reasons for my journey was to look for Manx
shearwater colonies in the cool northern islands. Eventually
I found some nesting on the steep cliffs of the off-islands of
Hestur and Koltur. Here in the late summer Faeroese men
collect the nestling sea-birds for food. Just before leaving the
Faeroes, almost by chance, I found it possible to take with me
an adult shearwater from a burrow on the Koltur cliffs containing a week-old chick. It had to stay in the box for three days
until I could get back to the *Primula*. Captain Ekholdt was
amused to find me returning on board with yet another shearwater, eight days after I had released the Skokholm shearwaters in these waters.

On reaching the Firth of Forth on the sixth day after I had

collected this shearwater from the wild cliffs of Koltur Island, I placed on its leg a band numbered RW7664, and released it over the sea near Edinburgh harbour.

I reached Skokholm two days later, and on the same night went to the village on the knoll and picked up both shearwaters which I had released twelve and eleven days previously on the journey north!

As for the shearwater from Koltur, in a week or so it had almost been forgotten. Then farmer Carl Niclasen, who had promised to look out for its return, wrote to me by the Koltur post-boat on 13 August to say that

The Skrapur [shearwater] returned to Koltur on 9 August, with ring on its leg numbered RW7664. I found the skrapur in the company of its young on that day. With good wishes from all at Koltur. N. C. Niclasen.

Carl had understood far more than I had supposed, and I had underrated his enthusiasm and tenacity. But nothing is too much trouble for the fine people of the little islands whose lives are regulated less by the monetary consideration (Carl would have been insulted had I offered him a cash reward for his labour in climbing down that cliff each day to look for the shearwater) than by the true spirit of kindness. To reach the shearwaters at all had been for me a matter of tricky rope-work upon a precipice. To visit that wild crag at night must have been even more difficult. That he recovered the bird at all so late in the season (a month after banding) and quoted the band number to prove it, was astonishing enough, without the pleasing evidence of his labour of love in the course of science and friendship.

These were the first of a series of homing experiments with Skokholm shearwaters, continued over several years by myself and other workers, the details of which have long been published in scientific journals. Some shearwaters were released far inland in England, and returned at top speed by the following night, proving an immediate orientation unexpected in a species which is normally never seen to fly inland unless storm-driven. Encouraged by this success we sent some still farther inland for release high up in the Swiss Alps; of these some orientated at once and duly returned, but some did not.

Two were sent 930 miles by air to Venice, and released in fine weather over a lagoon. They started off southwards for the open Adriatic, but one was presently seen to turn and rise up into the sky and fly westwards towards the high Appenine Mountains. Evidently it pursued a general direction overland for Skokholm, despite the attraction of the vast expanse of the Adriatic lying in the opposite direction. A fortnight later I picked this bird up in fat condition, in her burrow (A) in the knoll village. The other bird was not recovered until early next spring.

To return by sea all the way from Venice would have involved a flight of 3,700 miles, firstly south-east down the Adriatic, then south-west round the heel of Italy, then west to the Strait of Gibraltar, before finally turning north in the open Atlantic for Skokholm. To accomplish this distance in fourteen days would have meant an average speed of about 260 miles a day non-stop. But we ought to allow half of each day for resting and feeding, which means we must double the mileage per day, say 500 miles, or approximately a surface speed of above twenty miles an hour. Increase this speed to thirty miles an hour, to allow for natural deviation in flight, and the shearwater could just about have made it – but this presupposes it *knew* both the Adriatic and the Mediterranean seas so well that it could fly in a direction opposite to Skokholm for the first 500 miles! It would certainly not have time for random searching. But in fact this shearwater has never been known to enter the Mediterranean, let alone the Adriatic.

It was certain that the shearwater which flew towards the setting sun on the evening of its release at Venice, took a much shorter route (direct overland 930 miles to Skokholm). As it was seen to mount inland towards the mountains, we may suppose that it was guided home by that same innate direction-finding mechanism responding to the visual clues of a clear sky which had motivated the earlier, inland releases I have mentioned. My guess was that, after crossing the backbone of northern Italy, it may have diverted slightly from the straight 930-mile flight by the sight of the sea in the Gulf of Genoa, and flown down to rest and feed there. Once fully recuperated, it would again respond to the natural urge to return to mate and nest by heading for Skokholm. Guided by its direction-finding apparatus, it would next have flown towards home over the land mass of the southern mountains of France, and so reached the Bay of Biscay. Here it would be in familiar waters: hundreds of our banded shearwaters had already been recovered along all shores of the north coast of Spain and the west coast of France: records due largely to hunting by the Latin fishermen, who shoot the sea-birds both to eat them, and to determine if the birds have been feeding on their favourite food, sardines – and if so the fishermen set their nets accordingly.

The fat condition of the homing bird a fortnight after release at Venice was easily explained by a sojourn of probably several days among the sardines of Biscay! Indeed the recoveries of so many shearwaters, banded as adults at Skokholm over the years, in the Bay of Biscay in the summer months (April, 130 records; May, 44; June, 29; July, 33; August, 46) had been so remarkable that I was drawn to investigate the reason. I went to sea with the Biscay fishermen and witnessed the shooting. With the aid of French marine biologists I discovered that the inner corner of the Bay of Biscay is the nursery of the Atlantic sardine, the adult form of which is known as the pilchard – *Sardina pilchardus*. This fish spawns in the English Channel. The eggs float and hatch into tiny sardines which gradually swim southwards to winter in this nursery in the warmer waters close to Biarritz, St Jean-de-Luz and the Spanish–French frontier. In the following spring and summer the growing sardines move in shoals up the coast again towards Brittany, but may be two or more years growing into pilchards, before they penetrate the approaches to the English Channel. It is during their immature state, as sardines, that the shearwaters relish them, and the banding recoveries show that even when the adult birds are brooding eggs or feeding young at the nest on Skokholm, some fly all the way to Biscay – a distance of between 300 and 600 miles – to gorge on this favourite food. This is especially the case in the early part of the summer, when the small fry of other fishes is scarce in the cooler waters around Skokholm.

This long flight to feed on the fat oily young sardines also helped to explain the alternate shifts of several days of guard duty on and off the nest, egg and young chick.

The jig-saw of facts about the fascinating lives and habits of my ocean-going villagers from the knoll was falling into a comprehensible pattern at last. The homing experiments were concluded with some severe long-distance tests, which some individuals failed. Thus Baby, ex-wife of Adam, was sent from the village with seven other shearwaters by ship for release in the South Atlantic. The journey over the equator was too long; all the birds died en route. Similarly when two shearwaters were sent by ship to Boston, Massachusetts, they arrived in a weak condition, were released successfully, but were never recovered again.

Nevertheless, when, several years later, in two experiments, five shearwaters were sent by air direct to Boston airport, where they were released within two days of leaving their nest-burrows, one returned in $12\frac{1}{2}$ days and another in 14 days. This meant a flight of 3,050 miles over the uninterrupted, trackless North Atlantic. To have returned in that time the shearwaters averaged (in round figures) about thirty miles an hour (allowing half the time for resting and feeding, and adding one third to a surface speed of about twenty miles an hour for natural deviation in flight), a speed which hardly admits time for random searching for the way home.

It was noticeable in all these tests that when release occurred on a dull overcast day of poor visibility and mist, with no sun visible, the shearwater invariably circled the point of release as if lost; and in most instances the return was much later (some not at all) than over the same distance when the release was made in clear weather. These birds were lost, and doubtless flew aimlessly until they could re-orientate when the sky cleared and the heavenly bodies became visible.

These experiments did not explain, but only proved the existence of, a biochemical mechanism in the tiny brain of the shearwater which enables it to orient, apparently by the celestial signs, and return when transported up to two or three thousand miles from home in closed boxes. This extraordinary ability to know where it is on earth at any given moment or place within hundreds of miles of its geographical range has now been shown to be true for many migratory animals, from whales to birds, also some insects, and possibly some fishes. But how? In many ingenious new tests on wild birds, captured on migration and placed in enclosures, it has been proved that unless day migrants can see the sun (or the sun's position behind light cloud) they are disorientated and cease to migrate. This has been additionally confirmed by placing day migrants in a building lit solely by a bright lamp, simulating the sun. When this lamp was moved, the birds moved to take up a heading in their correct migration direction by the artificial sun, not by the real sun, which they could not see.

Equally birds which migrate at night do not orient accurately unless they can see the pattern of the major stars overhead. This was proved by tests on inexperienced young warblers during their autumn migration, which were placed in a planetarium the dome of which was illuminated with a faithful replica of the night sky and the major stars – correctly positioned as at that moment of night in the locality where they had been reared. When the cage containing the restless migrants was uncovered the birds at once oriented towards the south, endeavouring to take off on that bearing, their normal autumn direction. The cage was once more covered, and the planetarium sky with its imitation constellations revolved through ninety degrees until the southern stars were in a new and false position – true north by the compass. The warblers, as soon as the cage was uncovered, headed north, facing the southern stars. They continued to face the southern (imitation) stars no matter what the position of the false sky. When the planetarium was clouded over, with a diffuse light hiding the stars, the warblers moved about at random. When two young warblers, reared artificially indoors, were allowed to see the real stars for the first time in their lives they made initial headings in the correct migration direction. Finally, when these warblers were flown south in closed boxes by plane to south-west Africa, where the species normally spends the winter, their first reaction, on being exposed to the sky there, was to face southwards (to resume what might seem to them to be an interrupted migration?); but as soon as they 'read' the African sky correctly they settled down quietly as if they recognized from the celestial pattern that they had arrived in their winter quarters.

'The celestial pattern.' That bothered me a good deal, because, like the ever-moving sun by day, the celestial pattern at night is always moving, hour by hour. True, the North Star is virtually fixed, and the dome of heaven revolves around it in our northern hemisphere. But what of these young warblers, which must read a totally different celestial pattern, for they would no longer see Polaris once they had crossed below the equator? The same query applies to young Hoofti, of whose lone migration we were at last, through the banding of thousands of young shearwaters at Skokholm, getting a true picture. We now knew that immediately on reaching the water alone in the autumn the young bird swims vigorously away from the land and works its way southwards. If the weather is windy, this helps the young shearwater to gather his wings and start flying. It does not necessarily feed since it still carries enough body fat. But if equinoctial gales strike the Welsh coast at this time many of our banded shearwaters, feeble on the wing, are battered to death in the surf, or blown far inland. Those which survive fly on, alone, southwards via the Bay of Biscay, passing along the coast of Portugal, then across the equator, until they reach winter quarters off the east coast of South America. Banding returns at that season show that the majority of recoveries there are along the coasts of the Argentine, Uruguay and southern Brazil.

Some of these young shearwaters have flown very rapidly to winter quarters. One banded Skokholm youngster travelled 5,350 nautical miles in only 16½ days, in the fastest long-distance migration ever recorded; this represents an average speed of over 324 nautical miles a day, which would allow little time for rest and feeding! It might have been even faster, since it is believed that this bird, found dead on the Santa Barbara shore of Brazil, had probably died two or three days earlier.

Of course it must be an ideal life, living in perpetual summer simply by flying over the rim of the world! But to be able to find its way unaided by the adults, to leave behind the guidance by night of the North Star and its surrounding constellations, for the less vivid guidance of the Southern Cross and sky patterns, and of the low autumn arc of the sun in the northern hemisphere for the high spring arc of the sun in the South Atlantic by day, seems to me to argue that the tiny brain of the young shearwater is packed with the most extraordinary sensitive astronomical sextant-chronometer for navigation purposes? Or what?

Confusing this picture is the fact that the moon and the planets can hardly be much use as guides, bright though they are, to a migrating bird, because, compared with the sun and the stars, their motions, changing nightly, are far too erratic and wandering in the sky. So if a bird really does steer by sun and stars, it will have to ignore the moon and planets?

How can this be? I must go back to watching more closely the young fledgling shearwater. I must remember that it has never seen its parents clearly, in the darkness or twilight of the deep burrow. Nor has it yet seen the stars or the sun. Yet I am expected through the evidence of these homing experiments and banding returns to believe that it will be able to steer by these heavenly signs?

Study of periodicity and rhythmic activity in animals, particularly insects and crustaceans, has shown that they are born with an acute sense of time, that some order their lives on sun (day) time, some on sidereal (star) time, and some (marine organisms) on tidal (lunar) time. Somewhere in the brain they possess an internal, biological clock; in the cockroach it has been located in tiny cells within the nervous cortex, and this clock has even successfully been transplanted to work in the cortex of another cockroach.

But it appears that the tiny clock does not begin to work properly until the organism is exposed to light. The classic example is the fruit-fly: if reared in total darkness from egg to adult it is quite disorganized; but if the larva is permitted one or two brief flashes of light, imitating the dawn, at least three days before the perfect fly is due to emerge, the insect is able to set its clock accurately and emerge at the correct moment in the early morning for its tender body to absorb the dew – a process which will prevent desiccation during the drying heat of the sunlight.

How soon does the young shearwater acquire its time-sense (for it will need a very accurate internal clock if it is to steer by the ever-changing celestial signs)? It must be that it first sets its biological clock in that period when it emerges, alone, from the burrow at night, about its sixtieth day, and sits outside, resting, but flapping its wings at intervals? There is time to study, evening after evening for about a week, the whole dome of heaven (provided the night is suitable), and to memorize the position of the fixed stars, to check them upon the charts in the brain which it inherited with the genes from its parents? That is to say, for the short period of an hour or two over midnight when it dares to emerge, while the gulls are sleeping.

Watching one of these forlorn downy nestlings one dim midnight, while the soft clouds brushed past the jewelled Plough and Polaris above me, I imagined that if only it could reason out its problem, as I was trying to, it might think something like this: 'My parents have deserted me, and gone far southwards – I know that instinctively. Fortunately I did inherit from them the general know-how to follow; its in my brain – if only I can sort it out. Let me see, when I reach the sea I must head towards the correct star pattern, which I can find in the chart-room somewhere in my skull, for each hour of migration southwards. So my back will be to the North Star which is just above me now – that's certain, for a start. I have a reliable chronometer in my light-sensitive biological clock, which was correctly set by local solar time as soon as the first flash of daylight reached me down the dim corridor of the burrow (or maybe by star time when I first emerged the other night?). You may not believe it, but with the set of charts of celestial patterns in my brain I can interpret every movement of the sun or major stars each hour of my migration, and with my internal clock I can compensate for the movements of these heavenly bodies so as to keep on a straight line southwards. (But I don't pay much attention to the moon or the planets – they are too erratic!) Of course, when I go south beyond the Equator I shall lose my old friend the North Star, but I shall recognize other bright stars which will rise to guide me by night; and in my brain my astronomical charts of the South Atlantic will also warn me that the sun's arc will grow higher each day upon the sky. I shall easily recognize winter quarters when at last I reach them; not because the old birds will already be there (I wonder if I shall see my parents for the first time? I only remember them as voices in the dark, and as pipelines full of food for me), but because the information as to the position of winter quarters under certain celestial signs, as well as the physical appearance of the region, are both recorded in my brain, from the data I inherited in my genes from both parents. Finally, just at this moment I have an overwhelming desire to fly south, to beat my wings and escape the northern hemisphere and approaching winter, and this impulse to migrate is also genetically determined for me.'

Quite a performance – from innate wisdom! Not of course in so many anthropomorphic thoughts or by conscious planning; but yet the result is the same. From many ingenious tests we know that although they carry this 'sky-compass' or programmed computer in their head migrating birds are not guided by any form of the earth's magnetism. The experiments I have described suggest that they navigate over vast distances by an inherited knowledge of the celestial patterns along the traditional route. This is made all the more acceptable, I consider now, by the fact that most species migrate by the shortest route, i.e. in a straight line (unless temporarily thrown off course by strong winds) between their summer nesting grounds and their winter quarters. Any straight line extended far enough over and parallel to the surface of the earth will automatically complete a circle (known as the Great Circle) of the same length as the equator.

In following a Great Circle the migrating bird may be guided by the set apparent movements of the sun, or of the star patterns, which occur hour by hour, day and night, season by season, throughout the year. Those set patterns which occur during the precise hours of the day or night when the bird is migrating along its Great Circle voyage in spring or autumn have, it may be argued, become fixed in the genetic make-up of the bird during aeons of evolutionary pressures through which the powerful impulse to migrate was developed during the gradual changes in world temperatures (advance and retreat of the polar ice-caps – which once covered Skokholm). It is true that the apparent courses of the sun and the major stars are not really fixed at all in the heavens, but so slowly do they alter that for man's navigational calculations they are regarded as static during each epoch. Any slight alteration takes a century of time, during which the visual changes could easily be registered in the genetical charts in the brain of the many generations of birds living through that ample period.

Farewell, then, Hoofti, may your long first flight under the stars and over the ocean from Skokholm, 6,000 nautical miles to the estuary of the River Plate, be a happy one. I hope I have unravelled a little of what goes on in that tiny head of yours! Forgive me if I have put there thoughts you never possessed. My critics will undoubtedly once more accuse me of anthropomorphism, and declare you are a mere machine, an automaton evolved by blind chance in the universal struggle for existence, that you no more than filled a niche awaiting an organism which could burrow under the earth, swim under the sea and fly from one summer to another, and live perpetually on little fishes. But is that adaptation not wonder enough? Ah, I have learned to respect and admire, even to love you, brave little bird that would peck my hand, determined to survive all hazards, when I came too near and interrupted that long soliloquy of your midnight watch, when you thought your strange thoughts, while the sea-wind tossed the fragments of baby-down still clinging to your glossy new feathers. For you have taught me a little honest truth, and stirred my imagination to decipher a little of the natural law; and I find no evil in you and your ways, but only much beauty.

I have wished you good fortune; but very many of these young shearwaters die in their first year, and probably two-thirds before they reach maturity are killed from various causes, some taken by gulls on their way to the sea, some by equinoctial storms before they cross the equator. But thanks to the efforts of many observers at Skokholm of late years, in banding thousands of fledglings at the Hoofti stage, we now have a very fair knowledge of their survival rate and when they first return to the island where they were born.

From these published records it is clear that very few return to Skokholm in their first year, to be more exact only about one in 200. Instead, most of the surviving yearlings seem to stay at sea, and in summer move north as far as Bermuda, a few even to the Newfoundland coast. The first return of young birds in any numbers occurs in June and July when they are two years old. I would often find these adolescents exploring then, somewhat timidly, perhaps excavating a rabbit-scrape, but not usually penetrating far underground. They are beginning the necessary process of familiarizing themselves with the terrain and with other shearwaters of like mood and age, ready for breeding in the years ahead.

In their third year they return much earlier, from April onwards; and these individuals are more determined to stake a claim to a burrow. In doing so, they often clash with the old-established breeding birds, the rightful owners, but as already mentioned are usually driven out. In some instances, where an old bird has died from various natural causes, a three-year-old may take his or her place as a partner, thus fulfilling a useful function. The three-year-olds are a reservoir for this purpose, moving around from burrow to burrow, seeking entry, filling up gaps in the population, and digging new burrows of their own. They are courting, sweethearting. They sit together in couples, talking much, necking each other. But the females at this age, although their gonads are partly developed, do not lay an egg. Many begin laying in their fourth year, and both sexes are certainly fully mature and usually established in homes by their fifth summer.

Competition for the safe nesting recesses is severe at Skokholm, with the great increase in shearwaters under total protection, and some females may be forced to drop their egg in the passage to an occupied burrow or even in the open. Competition for burrows may also be one reason for Skokholm-born shearwaters visiting other west coast island colonies; certainly there is some interchange, mostly of banded Skokholm shearwaters turning up on neighbouring Skomer Island, or Copeland (N Ireland), Saltee (S Ireland), Bardsey (N Wales), Lundy (Devon), Annet (Scilly Is), and Ushant (Brittany); but also to a minor extent vice versa. These wanderers have sometimes been banded as full-grown at Skokholm and recovered a few days or weeks later on another island. In contrast those banded as nestlings have not been recaught on another island earlier than three years, and up to eight years, later. These are the colonists, overflowing from crowded Skokholm, and now breeding in their adopted home, many miles from their place of birth.

How long may the shearwater live, once it has survived the hazards of growing up, and has settled down to permanent breeding quarters? Since banding has proved that the female does not lay her first egg until she is four or five years old, we can calculate that Caroline, at the end of her eleventh breeding season, could not be less than fifteen years of age; she may have been several years older, for she was a strongly established householder in the village when I first banded her. Unfortunately, the first bands I used at Skokholm were of soft aluminium, their numbers were often obliterated and useless for identification after two years, so that I lost many as known individuals, and was soon obliged to place a new band on each villager in each spring in order to maintain continuity of identity.

With the new tougher metal band it is not necessary to re-band the shearwaters more often than every third year. From year to year in the marked burrows of the knoll village I found that about 90 per cent of the established breeders returned, despite the interference my frequent prying caused. In a larger group of 160 adult shearwaters breeding in study burrows, 1963–5 at Skokholm, M.P. Harris found that an average of 94.5 per cent survived to breed in the year following their marking at the nest.

For a small bird the shearwater has an excellent expectation of life once it is an established breeder. Studies of other seabirds which lay only one egg have shown a similar high adult survival rate: fulmar petrel, 93 per cent; short-tailed shearwater, over 91 per cent; royal albatross, 97 per cent; gannet, 94 per cent. But, except where a species is definitely increasing, to remain static in numbers it must have an average overall mortality equal to its rate of replacement. It has been calculated for instance that in the grey seal, which like the shearwater begins to breed at four or five years of age, and has only one pup annually, about 60 per cent die in their first twelve months. The mortality drops steadily in the succeeding four to six years of immaturity, to less than 10 per cent once breeding is established. One wild grey seal which we branded as a pup has lately been seen alive and well twenty-one years later (in captivity this seal has lived over forty years).

The shearwater has a similar high mortality in its first year; then follows the same pattern of longevity.

Caroline's record of sixteen years (five immature, eleven

breeding) has since been eclipsed by new records at Skokholm. Individuals, banded and re-banded, have proved that, like the seal, the shearwater can remain healthy and breeding up to at least twenty years of age and probably longer.

7 Puffins

The hedge-walls which divide the more level eastern half of the island into little fields had become bird sanctuaries. Originally they had been constructed simply, beautifully, by the men who had first farmed the island with plough and cattle, way back two hundred years or more. First, a ridge of earth some three to five feet wide was thrown up by digging trenches each side. All loose stones were gathered from the surface of the land and, with those turned up in ploughing, used to build a dry wall each side, care being taken to place the largest stones and boulders (known locally as grounders) at the foot, in the bottom of the trenches. Above these the next largest stones were laid, then courses of the smaller slate-like red sandstones, one above the other, each row slanted in a direction opposite to the next, forming an attractive herring-bone pattern.

The topmost layer was of heavier stones projecting slightly to keep farm stock in and rabbits out. These hedge-walls were last regularly maintained by the good farmer Captain Harrison (see page 175). Earth and stones falling into the ditches were restored, and the ditch each side annually cleaned by throwing the spoil back on top of the wall. Furze and thorn were encouraged to grow along the crown of the wall.

At that time sea-birds were much scarcer. They were caught for baiting lobster-pots, and the eggs and young birds eaten for food. Fisherman Jack had demonstrated to me how in the past he, and other fishermen, had taken them by setting rabbit long-nets along the cliffs at dusk; in the morning dozens of shearwaters and puffins and a few gulls were tangled in the meshes. But the taking of sea-birds is centuries old. George

Owen in an old book – *Description of Pembrokeshire* (1603) – describes the small islands of Pembrokeshire as the chief nursery of the sea-birds which 'are ripe about mydsomer, at which time they become flushe [fledged], and are taken being ready to forsake their nestes'. He specially mentions 'the Puffine, a bird in all respectes bredd of byrdes of his kinde by layeing egges feathered and flieing with other birds in the ayre, and yet is reputed to be fishe, the reason I cannot learne'. (Probably because to call a sea-diving bird fish meant that it could be eaten as such in Lent!) They were taken in nets, and also pulled out of their nesting holes with a *barbelé*, a rather diabolical instrument which I found local rabbit-trappers still used – there were several lying about Skokholm on my arrival. This consisted of a flexible stick or wire with a small barb at the end. It was thrust into the burrow until rabbit or bird was reached, then turned around until the fur (or feathers) and flesh were tightly screwed around the barb and the victim could be drawn forth. (I found the Maori 'mutton-bird' hunters still using a similar screw-stick to take burrowing shearwaters in the off-islands of New Zealand.)

Captain Harrison's daughter Mrs Folland had told me that the sea-birds were not abundant in her youth spent on Skokholm; but that as soon as the island was abandoned on her father's death, the trappers had begun to make breaches in the hedge-walls each winter so that the rabbits could have more places to breed. The dry earth inside was ideal for burrowing and shelter; and year by year the hedges became more riddled with holes. No longer troubled in the summer save by occasional marauding fishermen, the shearwaters and puffins also increased and moved in behind the rabbits each spring; they were gone by the time the trappers returned in the autumn.

Mrs Folland remembered listening, too, to the dainty little storm-petrels which purred at night in the hedge-walls. They could be heard on calm nights singing in the garden wall. They were small enough to squeeze between the stones, but they did no damage, laying their egg on the bare earth in a recess they scraped a little way behind. Her father would never molest them. As a retired master mariner he was unwilling, even fearful, of disturbing Mother Carey's Chickens. There is a tradition that each storm-petrel embodies the soul of a human drowned at sea. As I have myself seen, it flies closest to a ship in stormy weather. Its appearance then, with frail hovering flight, is regarded as a bad omen by the superstitious sailor.

Be that as it may, when I first came to Skokholm I found plenty of storm-petrels in the smaller cracks of the broken hedge-walls where rabbits, shearwaters and puffins competed for living room. There were even petrels in the outer walls of the derelict house. These nocturnal sprites I intended to study, too, for almost nothing was known of their life history.

As for the puffins, I have already described how they swarmed everywhere on my first visit. They were even sitting in a row along the ridge-pole of the house. 'No, puffins never came near the house,' Mrs Folland declared later when I told her this. 'I never saw them on the hedges either. There were no holes for them – just very few along the cliffs, mostly in rock crevices. I never went out to Grassholm, but I remember my father used to say it was swarming with puffins at that time.'

Grassholm is the little island of twenty-one acres, uninhabited, lying awash in the strong tides some nine miles west-north-west from Skokholm. A correspondent who read an article of mine about the gannets which breed at Grassholm wrote to say that

In 1883 I was the guest of Mr Richard Mirehouse of Angle, who took us out in his yacht and landed us at Grassholm for the night. In those days there was only a small colony of gannets, about twenty nests, not more, but the puffins were there in their thousands. We were hard put to find a bit of ground clear of puffin-burrows on which to erect our very small tent, but having, as we thought, done so, we put the tent up. At about 3 a.m. I was awakened by a curious grunting sound under my ear, and on removing my pillow there was Mr or Mrs Puffin, with a very grieved expression sitting at the entrance of a burrow. I made the *amende honorable* by clearing a way to the entrance of the tent, down which the aggrieved party attempted to make a dignified exit. I mention the above to give you an idea how thick the puffins were on the ground in those days.

In 1890 photographers visited Grassholm, took pictures and estimated that there were over 'half a million puffins' breeding. They had completely honeycombed the peaty surface. In succeeding years rain and wind caused the undermined hay-stack to collapse above the bare rock – for there is no soil beneath the accumulation of centuries of fescue grass roots. The great puffin slum became uninhabitable; and many thousands must have moved to Skokholm in the next forty years, finding conditions for colonizing ideal with the departure of the Harrison family. When in June 1934 I camped on Grassholm with Julian Huxley with the object of filming the gannets, now increased to 5,000 pairs, we had no difficulty in finding space for our tent. Green grass had grown over the holes and hummocks of the mighty puffin city of half a million, and only a few dozen survivors lurked on the edges of the cliffs.

This explained why Harry and I, on that first visit to Skokholm had been able to estimate some 40,000 puffins present. Most numerous of the birds to be seen by day, they were thickest in the evenings, when their sociable parading on the hedge-tops and the outcrops of rock amused us to laughter. I looked forward to a close acquaintance with these charming birds whose appearance and behaviour Harry had likened to that of stout convivial aldermen in evening dress, complete with scarlet nose and spats. The bird books contained virtually no information on their breeding biology, incubation, fledging, migration.

On my second, brief, visit in August most of the puffins had flown, and there was none to be seen when I took possession in October.

That winter, in my enthusiasm to be self-supporting in garden produce, I made and fixed a gate to the old garden in front of the house. I refaced the sides and top of the surrounding hedge-walls to prevent the entry of rabbits. I dug the soil deep, removing the bracken roots and destroying completely the system of ground burrows excavated by the rabbits and birds over the years since Bulldog Edwards' young wife last tended the garden. For a moment I had forgotten the puffins which had nested in the holes on top of the garden wall.

In February and March, between intervals of dismantling the wreck of the *Alice Williams*, I had planted potatoes, broad beans, lettuce, peas, and other vegetables, and herbs. The spring sunshine burned strongly down upon the sheltered enclosure. With the mild March rain, neat green lines appeared along the seed rows. Late in March the first small summer migrants arrived. Wheatears flicked their white rumps along the garden wall, and a chiffchaff sang its evocative notes in a sunny corner.

On 3 April the usually stoic Jack rushed into the Wheelhouse as I was preparing our food at midday, shouting so loudly that I was alarmed and dashed out to meet him.

'What on earth's the matter, Jack?'

But he was all smiles, and his innocent eyes were shining as he said, more soberly, as if a little ashamed of his exuberance: 'Puffins! Puffins!'

The long winter was indeed over. The flotillas of the puffins, returning from I know not what distant seas, had suddenly anchored in the island bays and creeks. Next day they began flying inland.

What joy! Welcome, painted, happy birds! I walked in the sunlight, greeting these merry companions of summer with a vast acceleration of my already high spirits.

Soon a small deputation of puffins alighted on the garden wall. They pattered along its length, peering and pecking comically at the smooth surface. They were so obviously nonplussed to find their burrows all neatly filled in that Jack and I burst into laughter. But how stupid of me, I thought; at least I could have left open the burrows on *top* of the wall, when rabbit-proofing the sides?

When the deputation moved off without attempting to open their old homes I hastily seized a pickaxe and probed a few holes in the crown of the wall. I must not spoil this splendid opportunity to study them at first hand and in comfort from the windows of the house which I was already beginning to repair.

But despite this hint the puffins never properly re-opened their buried homes on the garden wall. After furtive visits and some desultory scratching on the hedge-top they moved away altogether. Our frequent activity that summer in restoring the roof and walls of the house, and tending the garden was too much for them. And later I was to find that on arrival these adult puffins, already mated, preferred to repair and spring-clean old established burrows rather than dig completely new ones; there was no time to spare with the egg fast developing in the female early in April.

It was a busy summer; nor had I time to band and study the puffins, what with my own home-making and marriage on hand. But in the second spring I was able to begin watching a group of burrows on the lines adopted in the shearwater village.

Although so tame above ground that you could approach within a few feet of them, puffins proved to be little devils of non-cooperation in their burrows. They resisted handling fiercely, biting and scratching unmercifully with pincer bill and needle-sharp claws which drew blood. My first lot of marked birds either deserted their eggs or, rather mysteriously, the eggs disappeared, as if the owners had rolled them away out of my prying reach. In three seasons, out of twenty-four marked nests, I obtained only three full records of the incubation and fledging procedure.

Catching the puffin out of doors was however a remarkably easy and sportive operation, and we were able to band hundreds of them in this way. From time immemorial this bird has been fooled and captured in the open with net and snare wielded at the end of a kind of fishing rod. The inhabitants of St Kilda, up to the time of their leaving that remotest island of Scotland in 1930, used to catch them with nooses of hair attached to the end of a fifteen-foot pole. In the Faeroe Islands I saw how the fowler skilfully swept puffins up in a kind of long-handled lacrosse net as they flew along the face of steep cliffs. Rather a hazardous occupation, I thought, for sometimes in his over-eagerness the fowler himself tumbled over the cliff.

On my return from the Faeroes I invented a less conspicuous instrument – a nine foot long bamboo, with a three-foot length of strong plain wire attached, the tip of which I turned to form a miniature shepherd's crook. In practice, instead of waving the rod in the air (an action which often frightened the puffin away unless you were an expert fowler), you slide this weapon slowly along the ground until the crook can be slipped over the flat keel of the tarsus, or shank, of the bird's leg. It seems odd that the puffin, so shy and resistant to handling below ground, should permit the metal hook to touch its legs, but so it is. Often the puffin's curiosity is so strong that it will trot forward to examine the moving wire, even peck at and play with it, as it enjoys pecking and playing with loose objects it finds on the turf. It seems unable to associate danger of capture and death with the strange object – which, after all, *is* strange and unnatural in its normal environment.

Danger and death come to the puffin principally from natural enemies, from the sudden swoop of the predatory gull, or the arrow-fast stoop of the peregrine falcon. But when, as often happens, the great black-backed gull has successfully ambushed a puffin by lying in wait at the entrance to its burrow, the neighbour puffins watch the struggles of the victim and its subsequent evisceration without apparent concern. They have seen this sort of death before and it has never hurt them. 'Silly idiot,' one could imagine them saying (as we would comment on someone careless enough to be knocked over by a bus), 'Why didn't he take care to see there was no gull about before leaving home?' And they move only a little distance away from the gull. They make no attempt to combine and drive their foe away, as certain mammals and birds will do when one of their number is attacked. Instead in a short time they lose interest in the gruesome meal which their enemy is enjoying.

In my hand (carefully gloved) what a handsome, astonishing bird! Strange to realize that the rainbow-coloured beak, which contains the nostrils, is also a false nose. Much of it, as well as the vivid orange rosette or wattle of flesh around the mouth, is moulted at sea late in the autumn. So, too, the clown's make-up of grey wattle triangle above the eye, the rectangular pad below it, and the wagon-red of the eyelids: all these adornments are discarded at sea!

What is the meaning of this extraordinary painted visage? Both sexes have it, and except that the male is usually slightly larger you cannot tell them apart in the field. So then, it must be that their handsome faces induce mutual admiration which, kept thereby at a high pitch throughout the period they wear these adornments, maintains the pair-bond between the mated pairs for long enough to rear the chick. The puffin is a silent bird, but forever billing and cosseting, and if the amorous cock bird, gazing with love upon his mate, could only speak aloud, perhaps he would say, even more sincerely than Burns:

> As fair thou art, my bonnie lass,
> So deep in luve am I;
> And I will luve thee still, my dear,
> Till a' the seas gang dry.

For my banded pairs proved faithful to home and spouse. They returned year after year to the same nest burrow, there to meet, and greet with nose-rubbing, the same mate as the year before. They might be separated on their winter travels – I could not know – but otherwise 'as long as one shall live, etc.', applies with equal force to the puffin as to the shearwater (and I found the same endearing trueness to home and mate in the storm-petrel). In monogamous species, where the sexes are outwardly identical and display is reciprocal, male and female, once paired, remain lifelong partners (with just the rare exception of divorce and re-marriage to prove the rule).

On arrival at the end of March the puffins settle in rafts on the sea along the island shore. They indulge in the typical display and courtship ceremonies, later to be observed on land. It is really a sorting and reunion of partners, before going ashore. There is occasional fighting, but in general the gaudy bill is used less for inflicting wounds than as a flag to signal emotion, to warn off, to appease or to invite, as the occasion demands. It is opened to display the conspicuous yellow mouth in a long yawn which signifies preparedness to attack if the other fellow does not clear off. All puffin behaviour is diverting to witness; even the mating, which takes place in the water. The male balances perfectly upright for a few seconds on the tail of the female, whirring his wings in an absurd fashion so as to maintain position and lighten his weight, and so save her from sinking below the waves.

Suddenly, as by an order-in-puffin-council, after two to seven days of this courtship, mating and staking out of claims to burrows, the entire population deserts the island, usually for a period of the same length. It looks as if during that first invasion none of them has fed, that they need to return to their fishing grounds to recuperate far at sea.

The local fishermen used to declare that the sudden co-ordinated arrival and departure of the puffins was ordered by decree of a King of Puffins. Belief in co-operation between puffins was also strong in the Faeroe Islands, where the fowlers insisted that it was not cruel to kill adult puffins in the breeding season because 'there are seven grown puffins to every hole with one young bird. Imagine how difficult for the fowler to catch in his net all seven adults from one burrow. It is not possible – there are always some old ones left to feed the baby.'

The basis for this plausible but erroneous belief may lie in the fact that from midsummer onwards the adult population of puffins is doubled by the appearance of many full-grown but immature birds returning late for the 'sweethearting' and hole-visiting ceremonies (in the same way as immature shearwaters, already described) in preparation for breeding in the years ahead.

In my marked burrows the single large white egg was laid between 24 April and 16 May. Examined in a strong light the egg shows a dry limy surface with a zone of faint lilac or mauve spots around the largest diameter. Now most hole-nesting birds lay pure white eggs, for these are easier to see in the twilight, and protective colouring is of no advantage in such a safe situation. But most birds nesting in the open lay protectively coloured and marked eggs. The puffin's egg was a puzzle, made more complicated when I found that, instead of having one large incubation spot like the shearwater, the puffin has two small ones, one under each wing. Possibly, I thought, away back in time, the puffin, like the gulls today (which have two or three brood spots to incubate two or three eggs), laid two or more protectively coloured eggs in an exposed situation, such as a cliff ledge. My hypothesis was the simplest I could think of: it provided that those puffins which first hid their speckled eggs in crevices and burrows were the most successful in rearing their young. As they dug deeper into cover of rock or soil, the need for a camouflaged egg gradually faded – and so did the markings. Finally those two brood spots, but only one egg – how did I explain that? I did not, except to consider somewhat lamely that in the darkness of the burrow it proved easier to find and care for one egg, and of course it is always easier to rear one chick than two.

The puffin has not got rid of its surplus brood spot yet, nor has the egg lost all its colour even if it has grown as large as two small ones. But (I conjectured) at least the puffin now has one advantage over birds nesting in the open, which dare not leave the eggs unguarded; the puffin can, and does, leave the egg for long periods when the mood of the parents is to indulge in their favourite pastime – a sociable stroll or a joy-flight in the windy sunlight.

Like the shearwater pair, the mated puffins shared the incubation in shifts, but of hours, not days. The egg hatched in a shorter time – an average of forty-two days, and this despite the considerable period of daily chilling when the old birds were enjoying the post-meridian assembly. However, day temperature in the burrow was fairly high in May and June, and obviously no harm was done; possibly some benefit was derived from the regular cooling of the egg?

Whenever I could I tried to record the behaviour above ground by watching banded individuals, from a permanent hide I had erected in a populous cliff-edge colony. In my note-book I christened the male Frater and his wife Cula (from the scientific name *Fratercula*). Frater proved as uxorious as any other husband ought to be. He nuzzled and walked with Cula whenever she appeared outside the burrow at intervals during incubation. He put up a great show of affection and busyness.

'Marvellous day, my dear,' he seemed to be saying to her with his nodding flicking bill. 'Never fear, I've been strictly on guard at our front door every minute. And when are you going back to our beautiful egg?' 'As soon as I have stretched my legs. Excuse me, Frater, I am just going to the lavatory for a moment.' And, having decently walked a little way off, and defaecated well clear of the front lawn, she came back, went close to his face and seemed to whisper (although not a sound could I hear): 'Isn't it your turn on our beautiful egg, my dear hubby?'

'Oh, very well, I'll come along, bother you.'

Sometimes both would be below, but although he did some work there, she seemed to take the major share of the incubation. Frater preferred to stand watch outside for most of the time.

Both he and Cula were as typically nosy as all puffins are. They were possessed by inquisitiveness. When one was below the other would sit near the doorway, head jerking around non-stop as it viewed in turn the sky, the sea, the ground, and the activity of other puffins in neighbouring burrows. This watchfulness was in fact a natural protection against surprise from its enemies. But it could not bear to be passively idle for long. It would begin to stroll around, pick up stick or stone, perhaps pluck some of the flowers and grasses protruding around the doorway to the burrow ('gardening', I called this in my notes). A long straw or a feather, perhaps brought in from the sea, was a special prize, and it would be carried around in the bill with an obvious air of triumph. It was certainly an object of envy, for a neighbour puffin would often run forward and try to snatch it. Then ensued a comical tug of war.

But almost all this activity was random. After one visit to a neighbour and a silent inspection close to her face, Frater was seen to peep into her doorway ('H'm, looks pretty slummy to me!'). She allowed the liberty, only raising her beak with an air of hauteur. Next he trotted to a clump of sea-campion and began furiously to pluck a nosegay, until his beak was full and his face half hidden behind the fragrant flowers. But he often collected a mouthful of material, flowers, dead grass, in this way; and although sometimes he took the load indoors, he invariably brought it out again (the nest recess was usually unlined, the egg resting on the bare earth). Then, with what seemed to the human watcher an attitude of despair ('After all that trouble, she didn't even say thank you!'), he might fling it away with a shake of his head.

All this playful displacement behaviour of the puffin is conducted in complete silence. Occasionally you may hear from deep in the burrow that yawning laugh already described, a long indrawn 'Ahr' followed by the complemental 'Harr!' as the yawn is expelled on the exhaust stroke of the lungs.

But the only sound normally heard above ground is the faint preliminary rusty-hinge creak or gurgle as the huge bill opens in the threat yawn; and the growl uttered during a fighting match.

Frater liked to push his bill against that of his wife, but she was not always in the right mood for affection. At times when she was incubating below, or absent elsewhere, he might trot over and invite a neighbour to relieve his tedium with a little 'necking'. In this game his bill would be thrust forward close to the ground, quivering and slightly bowed. If the other puffin was responsive, it too lowered its bill and came forward. Face to face, the swaying bills would meet and remain locked together. It was not a clashing or fencing, as it is sometimes described to be. The bills were tightly pressed side by side, and each bird seemed to be trying to get its bill under the breast of the other, which resisted by keeping its head down and gripping the turf with sharp claws.

Any bout of mutual billing immediately excited neighbours, who would close in rapidly and form a ring of spectators. It was delightful to watch the vulgar craning of these bystanders, and the sudden awareness of the actors that they were being observed. The performance would stop. The pair might raise their neck feathers slightly like outraged cocks, and yawn threateningly, or one of them might make a lunge at the nearest spectator who had dared to breathe down his neck. If the pair continued billing the spectators would invariably become more excited and try to join in. This automatically broke up the game, and might end in a mêlée between the billers and the intruders.

In fighting the combatants would grab each other's mandibles and, thus clinched, would slash at each other with wings and claws, rolling on the ground in a confused heap. They might continue to roll until they tumbled over the edge of the cliff, when they would separate in mid-air. Or they might disengage, face each other, gape and clinch again. The fight would end with one party sidling away, hackles raised in a not undignified retreat ('That'll learn you not to interfere!').

In spite of the formidable bill and claws, fighting never resulted in more than superficial damage to the combatants. But fighting too, like billing or any other untoward behaviour, always drew a crowd of spectators. Often I saw neighbours run up to Frater and Cula at the approach stage of their billing, and inhibit any love-making before it had hardly begun ('Scandalous! You can indulge such disgusting behaviour down your own burrow, please!'). It was impossible not to smile at this inquisitiveness which suggested a spying spicy interest in each other's affairs. Yet, as nothing in nature is meaningless, this intense sociality resulted in a general prohibition of those activities which disturbed the peace and prevented the full enjoyment of the daily period of relaxation so beneficial to the health of a dense population. Idleness and yawning is highly approved in puffin society.

I never discovered whether puffins made love in the dark warm matrimonial home under the ground, but I would not be surprised. There were many things I did not know. Since they did not converse much, I wondered how mates identified each other below ground. By scent (its said that most birds have a poor olfactory sense)? Or just by subtle individual differences in behaviour, gait (the confident walk of a proprietor), and perhaps faint vocal sounds I could not catch as I strained my ears to the ground above the burrow?

Puffins are day birds. Only at night are the pair quietly at home, going to bed decently at dusk and sleeping until the first flush of dawn.

Despite the chilling of the egg while the adults are enjoying the wind and the sunlight over the joyous assembly period, hatching success is high. H. Dickenson opened sixty-nine previously undisturbed burrows at Skokholm and found an average of 96 per cent with chicks, and only 4 per cent with failed eggs.

As soon as the egg hatches in June, one or other of the parents remains on duty guarding the chick for a day or two. But the young puffin, unlike the young shearwater, is lively and active at birth, and can soon walk about. Protected by a thick coat of soot-coloured down, with white breast, it hardly needs the warmth of the brood patch under the parental wing. Both adults are quickly engaged in foraging for little fishes. They stuff the nestling with four to six full beak-loads of these during the day. Depending on the size of the little fishes and sand-eels (*Gadus*, *Clupea*, and *Amnodytes*), which grow larger through the summer, convenient to the increasing capacity of the young sea-birds, the puffin can catch and hold a remarkable number in its bill at one time, assisted by the rows of backward-projecting spines in the roof of its mouth.

Certain lazy herring gulls at this season sit around the puffinries, awaiting the return of the parents laden with fish. As the puffin flutters down towards its burrow the rogue gull dashes forward, forcing it (not always successfully; a puffin previously robbed in this manner may be wary, and dive straight into its burrow) to drop its load on the ground. Anticipating this, I too have lain in wait, ready with a clod of earth to throw at the gull, and with a shout and a clap of hands to drive it away. I have then counted the fish dropped on the ground: the number in a beakload averages between ten and twenty, with one record of twenty-eight small fishes.

The nestling puffin is fed entirely on raw fish, which it takes direct from the adult, and gulps down whole. Such a bulky diet (in contrast with the predigested fish-soup, free of indigestible bones, fed to the baby shearwater) results in the evacuation of quantities of waste matter. But the nest is kept perfectly clean. The baby puffin soon learns to run to the entrance of the burrow, as did the incubating parent. But the chick does not venture all the way forth to 'the place without the camp'. It remains in the comparative safety of the doorway, and, turning round, squirts its faeces with considerable force into the open. Who taught the child this desirable habit of sanitation? (For otherwise if it fouled its own nest it must surely die of suffocation from ammoniacal fumes.) Did it copy the adult behaviour? One could be sure of the presence of a chick in a burrow by this circle of guano immediately outside.

Yet it is not always safe for the chick to perform this sanitary operation. The great black-backed gull, with its own chicks to feed, is alert to pounce on the unwary nestling if it can seize it at this awkward moment of turning its back. This powerful robber will walk very quietly over the ground of a puffinry, 'listening' for the sound of any bird or young rabbit approaching the surface, and if necessary will thrust its long beak swiftly inside the entrance. But, apart from gulls, the young puffin has little to fear from other islanders. I never saw a rabbit naturally enter a burrow containing a puffin, unless it happened to be an entrance to a large system of burrows. I believe that the sensitive nose of the rabbit must be aware from the smell of guano which holes are occupied by burrowing birds with powerful beaks. And the young puffin is just as courageous as the young shearwater in pecking vigorously at all visitors. Probably it may even drive away those adolescent puffins which begin exploring the burrow systems about this midsummer season.

By counting the number of puffins landing with fish over a measured area of occupied burrows for a whole day of twenty-four hours, we were able to determine that the growing chick receives its main meals – at least one from each parent twice daily – early in the morning, and in the evening. The peak of fish-landings was between 07.00 and 09.00 hours, and 17.00–19.00 G.M.T. Fishing activity dwindles during the afternoon, when the social assembly calls strongly to these gregarious birds; and it was diverting to watch those birds which brought fish home then, standing around with the beakload for perhaps as long as half an hour, torn between the desire to stay in the sun with the other members of the puffin club, and the need to feed the chick below.

(One could almost hear the silent conversation: 'She's got a very fine catch, hasn't she? But she's a bit stuck up about it, don't you think? I wonder how many in that lot?' 'Reckon she oughtn't to show off like that, leaving the poor kid hungry so long.')

If hungry enough the chick utters a steady cheeping note. It was laughable to see idle adults, attracted by this noise, peer into the burrow, two or three together, and listen, heads slightly cocked on one side. ('Ha, they're neglecting poor Percy. Shocking behaviour!') But these adults did nothing about it, rarely going farther than the doorstep; and hastily backing away when a parent arrived with a load of fishes.

At six weeks the nestling is very fat, well feathered, and dressed in black and white like the adult; but the bill is small and black, the face and legs dark and the wings not fully developed. It weighs approximately two-thirds as much as the adult when it is finally deserted.

In my first summer at Skokholm, I had noticed that, whereas those other auks, the guillemots and razorbills, attended their chick at sea, the young puffins always swam alone. Nor had I ever seen a young puffin walking about above ground in daylight. Then, finding one or two of these fledglings trapped in the garden after some windy nights in August, I knew they must be moving to the sea at night.

This was easy to observe. Strolling over the large puffinries in the midnight hours, I found several of the little chaps sitting about rather forlornly, quite alone, or walking unsteadily to the cliff edge. Not a single adult visible in the light of my torch. Only at rare intervals could I hear a mature groan from under the ground, mostly too deep for me to reach the groaner; but when I at last pulled an adult out, it proved to be an obvious visiting adolescent with bright plumage – about two or three years old.

The old breeders had all departed, to moult their faded and frayed plumage. They had flown far out into the ocean, (as they drop their quill feathers all at once, they need plenty of sea-room). I turned my attention to the behaviour of the tender fledglings.

Every one of these above ground was making its way to the sea, sometimes falling accidentally into a burrow, but if so pulling itself out with hooking bill and clawed toes and fluttering wings. On reaching the cliff edge it paused briefly before plunging downwards into the darkness over the sea. One hit a boulder audibly; but when I climbed down to see if it was dead, I found it no more than slightly dazed. Its thick breast feathers and light weight had saved it. It bounced away from my fingers when I released it.

I collected half a dozen. Thrown into the sea in the morning each fledgling swam easily, making for the open Atlantic. When a great gull swooped it dived smartly, as the young shearwater does, and came up several seconds later many yards away.

By placing matchsticks upright in the mouth of burrows containing chicks of known age, I found that the parents gave up visiting and feeding their child about the fortieth day. The deserted chick, long active in trotting up and down the burrow on its sanitary strolls, did not venture out (and so push my matchsticks aside) until the fourth day, but one bird did not leave until eleven days had passed. No chick was ever found to return to its burrow once it had pushed the matchsticks over. The average fledging period was forty-nine days.

The exodus of the young puffins begins each night as soon as darkness falls in August: long before the gulls wake at dawn the fledglings have escaped from the land and all its dangers.

Banding of hundreds of puffins at Skokholm has now

proved that the young birds follow a pattern of migration similar to that of the shearwater. The fledged puffin, if it survives the normal high mortality of all young birds, swims much before its wing quills are fully developed and it is able to fly strongly. Unguided save by its innate navigational wisdom, it finally links up with the adults, which winter over a wide area of the cool waters of the North Atlantic, from Norway to Newfoundland, and south to the Strait of Gibraltar and Morocco.

Recoveries of these banded birds show that the majority of puffins remain at sea over the first and second twelve months of their lives. A few may return to Skokholm in their second summer, and many do in their third. The fourth summer is devoted to sweethearting and establishing a claim to a suitable burrow with a future mate. There is pair formation and much digging of new burrows but without producing an egg.

In the fifth year successful breeding takes place, and probably the puffin can live as long as the shearwater, and may not be old until it is twenty.

Which of these two birds, so evenly matched in size, won the frequent encounter and struggle when they met each other below ground? Sometimes I came across them fighting in the entrance to a burrow. In each instance the puffin broke off the struggle as they emerged, and the shearwater, disliking the light of day on land, retreated below. At other times I heard them scrapping deep under the ground, puffin growl matching shearwater scream. But in general there was an equal sharing of the island terrain between them, at least during the early years: the shearwaters dominated the interior and the west end; the puffins were most abundant along the cliffs and the east end. Undoubtedly the shearwater has the advantage of arriving first in spring, and although it laid its egg, on average, a day or so later than the puffin, it was nocturnal and therefore already in possession when the diurnal puffin walked into the burrow in search of a nesting site. But as to weapons, I myself preferred to be bitten by the thin hooked bill of the shearwater than by the power-driven forceps of the puffin's beak.

Alas, poor puffin. I must add the postscript that as the years passed by the huge estimated population of 20,000 pairs of 1928 has declined steadily, until today it is under 2,000. The loss suffered by this amusing bird has been the shearwater's gain: the empty puffin burrows have been taken over by the shearwaters, now treble their 1928 numbers. But we cannot blame the shearwaters for this decline of the puffins. It is much more certain that increasing pollution of the Atlantic seaway by tankers cleaning out their bilges has caused the severe reduction in the numbers of surface-swimming sea-birds, such as the puffins, guillemots and other auks, so noticeable today. We constantly find them dead or dying of the tarry filth on the coasts of Wales. Unlike the gulls and shearwaters, which fly over the waters in their search for food and are therefore able to spot and avoid oil slicks, the puffins and other auks live by diving and swimming, flying as little as possible, and thus they are more prone to be trapped by the floating oil.

8 Rabbits

By day my eyes were forever uplifted to register delight in the vivid moods of the sky and the sea, to watch the pageant of the diurnal birds and the wild flowers. But it seemed to me that my thoughts were frequently deep in the ground too, still puzzling over the affairs of the inhabitants of the bird and rabbit burrows, where by far the greatest numbers of the vertebrate subjects of my little kingdom lived.

As described in the historical chapter at the end of this book, I had unravelled something of the history of the exploitation of the rabbit since its introduction by man in late Norman times 600 years ago. But I had not yet sorted out the complex and intriguing situation caused by the return from their oceanic wandering of the huge fleets of shearwaters and puffins – about 100,000 strong, counting the non-breeding as well as the breeding adults – at a critical moment in spring swamping the rabbits which had commenced to breed in the long corridors and ample underground burrow systems where they had lived so comfortably over the five months of winter.

It was important to study how best I could harvest the rabbits without undue cruelty. I had planned never to use the horrible gin-traps again, but at the same time, in those early years, I needed the revenue from the rabbits. If possible I would exterminate them altogether. Not because I hated them – I was quite fond of rabbits, and had for many years kept them as pets, and bred them commercially on my mainland farm – but because I had plans to replace them with something more profitable and easy to control.

Many and ingenious were the plans I made, and some which others proposed, for wiping out the island rabbits. But all were to prove of no avail. And in the years since, in a long study of the animal, my admiration for its adaptability and resilience has only increased.

In my first winter we caught 2,415 rabbits by trapping, which I estimated to be about two-thirds of the population and equivalent to ten adults per acre. In the second winter, using ferrets, dogs, ordinary snares, humane snares, long-nets, shooting – everything we could think of, including wire-netting funnel traps into which we tried to drive large numbers at night – we caught 2,908. There were, it seemed to me, not very many left by that spring; and an all out effort in the third winter resulted in a catch of 2,785 rabbits.

It was interesting to find that just over 1 per cent of this total of 8,108 rabbits caught were abnormal, that is to say mutants:

> 36 with long hair ('Woollies' or Angora type)
> 28 black (melanic)
> 22 with white nose-blaze and saddle (Dutch type)
> 1 partial albino with black eyes
> 1 true albino with red eyes

Jack believed that these 'sports' were merely throw-backs to tame rabbits which must have been introduced in the past. I was not so sure; I had a feeling that it might have been the other way round: that these were naturally recurring mutants which, taken into captivity centuries ago, had been the progenitors of some of the domestic breeds – the Angora, black, Dutch and white varieties.

My first reason for wishing to exterminate the wild rabbits was to replace them with the domestic Chinchilla rabbits I had been breeding on my Monmouthshire farm. At that time one good pelt of this variety (which had been so cleverly evolved by line-breeders to resemble the fur of the real Chinchilla – a totally different, squirrel-like creature on the verge of extinction in the Peruvian Andes) was worth ten shillings. My simple argument was that if I could replace the wild ones with Chinchilla rabbits, fetching ten times the price I had been getting for the former, I would be financially very much better off. Moreover the Chinchillas' skins could be taken and prepared for market at leisure: I should not have the present anxiety of wild rabbits spoiling in the frequent delays, due to bad weather we had experienced in getting them to the mainland.

It did not work out that way. First, I failed to get rid of the wild rabbits. Second, when I tried out some of the Chinchilla rabbits in a rabbit-proof enclosure on the island, they did not thrive without expensive supplementary hand-feeding; moreover in grazing the pasture, contaminated with the natural parasites of the wild rabbits, the Chinchillas were prone to contract coccidiosis and other endemic diseases from which they died easily. Finally the market for rabbit fur at that moment – the depression of the 1930s – slumped disastrously.

My second reason for exterminating the wild rabbits was the intention to reserve the pasture for sheep, so much more easy to manage and involving no problems of winter-boating in stormy weather. So, when the Chinchilla experiment failed, I introduced a small flock of hardy Welsh lowland cross sheep. I gradually increased these to 100 ewes by the end of the third winter, having by then reduced the wild rabbits to their lowest numbers.

To be a shepherd suited my temperament, which was to observe and enjoy the natural scene. This was a happy time, making the daily round to inspect my flock, and to note down every bird and flower in my phenological record. I procured a sure-footed mountain pony stallion to ride, and a sheep-dog. The rams were not introduced until November, so that the ewes could lamb with the first flush of spring grass. And at first the sheep did well. The ewes reared an average of 1¼ lambs each.

There was plenty of grass as yet. The only anxiety was the lambing period. I found that I had to be alert for the ravens and great black-backed gulls. These hovered around like vultures in expectation of attacking the lamb if the ewe was weak and slow to protect it at birth; even if she was a good mother they would try to snatch the afterbirth before the hungry ewe herself (from an appetite which was also a protective device, since it removed the conspicuous evidence of her present vulnerability to predators) devoured it.

There was one disappointing feature in the existence of a large flock of sheep on a small island. They greedily browsed some of the scenically choice flowers which the rabbits would not willingly eat, such as bluebells, sea-campion and thrift (sea-pink). The dense masses of acres of these covering much of the island were no longer so spectacular, because the sheep had nibbled away so many of the flowering heads. Still, I suppose they were improving the pasture in doing this, and I ought to have been pleased – as a shepherd.

The remnant of the rabbits surviving the three-years' onslaught on their numbers were not dismayed by the competition from the sheep. Instead, I noticed that they were craftily breeding much earlier than usual, some of them even throughout the winter. They continued to multiply. Unfortunately it was no longer economical to market them. In the world depression, 1931 to 1936, the price of wild rabbits never rose above 2½d per lb. We did not trouble to ferry ashore those we caught.

If only (I fervently wished) those Norman barons had never introduced their conies to Skokholm! Of course they had had no thought of the disturbance to the ecology of the island the introduction would cause: destruction of the original flora, which very likely included trees and woody plants; and deterioration of the grazing for farm stock – the 'agistment' mentioned in their documents. Neither had they given thought to the ethical consideration, which was to trouble me: how to catch rabbits humanely, for if I did not succeed in reducing them each winter they would probably increase to the point of malnutrition and starvation – to say nothing of eating the pasture from under the very noses of the sheep which provided a substantial part of my income.

And that is what was happening. As the rabbits got the upper hand, the island pasture in winter became very bare, and I was obliged to hand feed the sheep for the first time, to strengthen them for lambing. The writing was on the wall.

In September 1934 I admitted defeat. I hired two barges and removed the whole flock in one operation. That winter I devoted to journalism, between visits to other islands than Skokholm.

Among the articles I wrote was one on my experience in trying to exterminate the island rabbits. This brought an unexpected and astounding offer from a scientist to do the job for me, and very quickly, if I would agree to the use of 'germ warfare'. Sir Charles Martin had had considerable success with the virus of myxomatosis upon rabbits inoculated and placed in small grass enclosures at Cambridge. Two artificial colonies of fifty-five and forty-four wild rabbits had been exterminated. Now he wished to try the virus on a larger population, well isolated from the possibility of infecting mainland rabbit warrens; and what better, he wrote, than remote Skokholm?

What better indeed! I knew nothing about the disease caused by the virus, nor indeed did Sir Charles know a great deal. But he was hoping to learn more. He was studying the virus on behalf of the Australian Government with a view to controlling the millions of the introduced European rabbit which plagued that continent. Apparently the virus was endemic and comparatively harmless in the South American rabbit, but when some domesticated European rabbits were imported into Brazil, they had contracted the disease. One strain of the myxoma virus proved to be 100 per cent fatal to European rabbits. They had virtually no resistance to the disease, which however affected no other animal; even the hare was immune. And although (Sir Charles wrote) its effects were unpleasant to the human eye, for the rabbit's head swelled and it became blind, the affected rabbit died in a very few days after the first symptoms were apparent. It was curious, he added in his letter, that myxomatosis in its latter stages seemed not to be painful; the appetite remained good up to the last moment, and probably the swelling of the head deadened the nerves, while the unaffected stomach still craved food.

Thus assured, and indeed quite excited at the prospect of returning to a shepherd life with no winter-starving rabbits to trouble my conscience, I gladly agreed. The sequence of events thereafter was the result of an extraordinary coincidence, due to ignorance of how the virus was conveyed from one rabbit to another. From his experiments with closely confined populations at Cambridge Sir Charles firmly believed that contact between individual rabbits was essential to the spread of the virus. Had he known that this was far from the truth he might have been much more careful in his trials at Cambridge in 1935; it was perhaps both a misfortune for the scientific evidence he was in search of, and good luck for the rabbits of England, that the virus had not escaped from his pens at Cambridge – as well it might have. Twelve years were to pass before the carriers of the disease were recognized.

Sir Charles came to Skokholm in the autumn of 1936 and again in the spring of 1937 and of 1938, to inoculate the rabbits with the most lethal strain of the myxoma virus. Altogether 145 were caught, marked, inoculated, and released at points widely scattered over the island. All the marked rabbits found subsequently had died of the disease, but only a few unmarked ones contracted myxomatosis and died. And in total result the virus had no appreciable effect on the now large population. Within a few weeks of each inoculation not a trace of the disease remained. It was a bitter disappointment to Sir Charles, and to me as would-be shepherd.

Because of this failure, no one was much interested in the results when they were published. The Australian government was probably the most disappointed of all concerned; but research continued on some Australian islands, again with little or no success. Then suddenly in 1950 the disease became big news, with the discovery that in river valleys the Australian mosquitoes were effective carriers of the virus.

At first it was supposed that the rabbits would swiftly disappear in Australia. But in fact, in dry areas without mosquitoes, myxomatosis was to prove a failure; and Australia still has a grave rabbit pest problem. However the reports of its success there induced a French scientist and virologist, Dr Armand Delille, in 1952, to introduce the virus to combat the rabbit plague within the 600 acres of his walled estate in the country west of Paris. Later I was to meet Dr Delille, who told me the whole story. Over 99 per cent of the wild rabbits had been killed by the disease in a few weeks of midsummer. When neighbours asked if they could have infective rabbits to start the disease on their rabbit-plagued lands, Delille had refused; but people had broken into his estate by night, and carried the sick rabbits away. He told me that the hunting fraternity of France, where the rabbit enjoys a close season, were very angry with him, and intended to prosecute him for his experiment which was to decimate the rabbit population of Europe so severely for many years to come.

(The case against Delille was brought to court, but failed on a technicality. It could not be proved that he had himself allowed the virus to escape from the walls of his estate.)

It is possible that my experience of the virus on Skokholm induced the Nature Conservancy, when myxomatosis appeared in wild rabbits in England, after the virulent outbreak artificially created in France, to invite me to study its progress and vectors in Britain. It had arrived in England in 1953, one year after its liberation near Paris.

I went to the scene of the first outbreaks (in Kent) of this disease which had so unaccountably failed at Skokholm. I noticed that both the freshly dead and the dying myxomatous rabbits were heavily infested with their natural flea (*Spilopsyllus cuniculi*). I collected live fleas from both and placed them in test tubes packed with rabbit fur. At a research laboratory between five and twenty-nine of these fleas were placed on each of five domestic and two wild rabbits. Some of the fleas had survived already for six days on the body of their dead host, but, kept warm in the tubes for a further two days in transit, they proved capable of carrying the virus over the eight days; and all seven rabbits died eleven to thirteen days after receiving the infected fleas. Sucked up with the blood of the rabbit, the virus is carried on the mouth parts of the flea, which acts as a hopping contaminated pin.

Myxomatosis had spread rapidly through the British Isles, carried not by mosquitoes, but by infected hopping fleas, and by farmers who deliberately transported diseased and dying rabbits to new areas. Probably wild birds also, feeding on infected carcases, carried many fleas to clean areas; I had noticed how the fleas would climb on to my clothing when I handled sick rabbits: for as each rabbit died in a warren, many of the fleas moved to the remaining live rabbits, which finally were swarming with hundreds of highly infective fleas.

At last the disease reached Pembrokeshire, and in 1955 crossed the sounds to the sea-bird sanctuaries, almost certainly on the bodies of gulls and buzzards returning to their island night-roosts after feeding on myxomatous rabbits on the mainland. The reason why the virus had failed when introduced at Skokholm by Sir Charles Martin eighteen years earlier suddenly became apparent when the rabbits on Skomer, only two miles as the crow flies coast to coast from Skokholm, went down with myxomatosis and were nearly exterminated, but those on Skokholm were untouched. For some reason not yet explained there are plenty of rabbit fleas on Skomer, but (despite much searching by myself and others) none has been found on Skokholm! Sir Charles, now an old man, learned on his deathbed why his choice of Skokholm for his experiments had been such an unlucky coincidence.

The rabbits at Skomer may have been about 20,000 strong when the disease struck, leaving probably less than half of one per cent of immune and resistant survivors (usual after a first epidemic). In the following summer the ungrazed vegetation grew tall and matted. Gradually the Skomer rabbits regained their numbers. But at the time of writing they have suffered two further epidemics of myxomatosis in twelve years, each less lethal than the preceding one, as the virus continues to weaken in virulence and more immune individuals occur.

Meanwhile the Skokholm rabbits have remained immune, fluctuating in numbers over the years for a very different reason. No fleas bother them. Nor is man any longer a nuisance, save occasionally to take one for the pot, or for science. He is simply an observer, studying how they are working out their problem of overpopulation – that same problem which is also a very real one for the human rabbit.

*

I must go back briefly to the last inoculations with the myxoma virus at Skokholm in 1938. On its failure in that year, I received yet another offer to attempt to get rid of the rabbits, by a new, humane method. This might have succeeded if the second great War had not intervened; but I am not sure.

The Universities Federation for Animal Welfare at that time were searching for a humane alternative to gin-traps for catching rabbits. UFAW had engaged with me and others in a public campaign to make them illegal (a campaign which did not succeed until myxomatosis and the virtual disappearance of the rabbit in Britain made their use unnecessary, and a new Pests Act was passed in 1954 prohibiting them altogether). UFAW arranged with me to demonstrate humane rabbit extermination, by the use of calcium cyanide in dust form at Skokholm. Blown through the passages of warrens by means of a hand-pump, the dust gives off the lethal hydrocyanic gas. As the dust emerges from exits in a warren, these are blocked so as to ensure concentration of the gas within.

Work began on Skokholm in the winter of 1938-9, when tests on rabbits in rock crevices and shallow holes proved that death occurred within a few seconds, the animals stretching out without excessive movement, and without screaming as they do when in distress. Next – a big job, requiring a party of men – all accessible holes on the island were closed. Many thousands of course were bird-holes only. As there were no birds below ground at that season all re-opened holes indicated rabbit activity. These re-opened burrows were fumigated and closed again. It was estimated that about 90 per cent of a possible total population of some 10,000 rabbits had been killed in the first gassing.

Holes re-opened in the next few weeks were again fumigated; but few were re-opened after that, except along the cliff edge. At the end of the winter, by the time the first shearwaters were returning to open their burrows, we calculated that only about 400 of the original 10,000 rabbits had survived, and most of these appeared to be rock-dwellers coming to the top of the island to feed at night from the tangle of boulders and talus below the cliff edge.

Proof of this success was forthcoming in the summer of 1939. White clover appeared where it was rare and stunted before, grass grew long and luxuriant, and in the home meadow we actually cut as much as four tons of hay from one acre. (The last hay I suppose had been cut by Bulldog Edwards some thirty years before.) Grass continued to grow, some of it smothering the rabbit-resistant wild flowers. We imported a hundred young sheep to graze it. We could win yet.

Alas, for the final success of extermination! We failed to reach and kill those last guerrilla rabbits hiding in the cliffs, though we hunted them all summer. UFAW laid formidable and expensive plans for the next winter, when the sea-birds had gone, which involved laying sheets of canvas over the cliffs and boulders, and pumping vast quantities of gas beneath. Even had we been able to carry out this project in the winter gales, which was extremely doubtful, I had a feeling that there would always be one or two rabbits left, lying up in some secret inaccessible place, until the last whiffs of poison gas had blown away on the wind.

Yet it was a near thing, the lowest point of population the island rabbits had ever reached. But as it happened the rabbits won – a little unfairly, I shall always feel. They had been saved by a madman. Hitler had really started his war at last. We had to leave the island.

On our return five years later, Skokholm had recovered its old pristine beauty. With its rabbits restored in numbers, it was bright with wild flowers again – the rabbit-resistant blue-bells, campion and thrift.

They had their uses, these rabbits! They kept the turf like a billiard-table for smooth walking. They dug burrows for the convenience of hole-nesting sea-birds. And although some birds liked the cover of thick vegetation for feeding and breeding, far more species preferred the wide open country. Their numbers actually increased with the increase of the rabbits. It might be declared quite safely that this little island of Skokholm contained a greater number of bird species and certainly a greater number of individual birds to the acre than any other spot in the British Isles – under my protection, but also largely thanks to the activities of rabbits!

*

The island rabbits are very tame in summer, tolerating a closer approach than is possible to mainland rabbits. Early in our life at Skokholm we had an unusual opportunity to ob-serve them as individuals. The new windows I had placed in the thick wall of the Wheelhouse were like the box at the theatre of a Beatrix Potter play. The rabbits could not see or hear us through the glass. We could study their personalities so amusingly revealed each day about the time they emerged from their burrows, which coincided with our midday meal (the Wheelhouse has remained a refectory to this day). It be-came our habit to linger over a cup of coffee, gazing upon rabbit society, pointing out to any friends or visitors some of our cony acquaintances: the old warrior buck with the torn ear, the doe with the white star on her forehead, the black doe who was so shy (as if she was conscious of a colour bar), and others distinguished by some physical or behavioural peculiarity. There was also one 'Dutch-marked' female wild rabbit which Ann had reared as a kitten, and which had now joined this community inhabiting the stretch of hedge-wall a few yards away from the windows of the Wheelhouse.

There was little time however in those first summers to do more than note down their behaviour and – from those killed – the period of the breeding season and number of young carried by does. But as these random observations accumulated they added up to a fair picture of their life history, and encouraged the fuller studies of later years.

In one experiment with the island rabbits I confined one group (Intensive Pen) in a wire-netted enclosure of one acre, and allowed them to increase to maximum numbers, thus simulating the crowded island condition in miniature. Alongside was another enclosed acre (Extensive Pen) in which I placed one buck and a doe, but I removed all their progeny as fast as I could catch them at weaning time. This Extensive Pen provided conditions of living space and abundant food resembling those following a crash of population after an epidemic. Each rabbit in these pens was marked with a number tattooed in the ear, as well as a conspicuous metal tag bearing the same number and pinned to the base of the ear. This study (which for convenience of all-the-year-observation took place on the nearby mainland) of the Skokholm rabbits continued over four years, and added much to our knowledge of individual behaviour. I can only summarize it very briefly here, adding thereto the results of work at Skokholm by others, particularly that of Hugh Lloyd of the Ministry of Agriculture.

Through centuries of restriction to a small island of 240 acres, and of adapting to its often harsh winter conditions, the rabbits have developed certain differences of appearance and behaviour. They are smaller than the average mainland rabbit, by a live weight difference of one-fifth lighter. The fur on the back is darker, due to a more plentiful admixture of the long black guard hairs overlying the browns of the body fur. They are more diurnal, appearing above ground from noon onwards.

They are more difficult to catch. Having no mortal enemies below ground they are, as we have seen, apt to remain there when chivvied by ferrets; they have long lost the instinct to bolt of their mainland ancestors introduced by the Norman barons six centuries ago (page 166). The (muzzled) ferrets we used were nonplussed by the failure of the island rabbits to bolt, and at last became bored with vain scratching at them and returned to the surface with their claws full of rabbit fur.

Gin-traps had not been specially efficient either. On hearing the screams of the first rabbits caught, most of the others would remain below until a few days later the trapper lifted his diabolical instruments. Old Dick had declared that trap-shyness was worse on the island than the mainland. Again, never having to run from foxes or other fleet-footed enemies, Skokholm rabbits were definitely – in Dick's words – 'lazy b—rs, them be too tired to run into a noose!' This was his explanation for catching so few in his wire snares.

Why, indeed, should the island rabbits run about? Where could they run to, on an island? Each was as happy as it ever could be in its own circle of territory, where it could enjoy the essentials of life for a rabbit – enough food and shelter in the first place, and companionship and sex satisfaction as secondary desires. The more you studied the social structure of rabbit society the more human it seemed to be! The significant difference, a priest once told me, was that, clever though they are, rabbits have no souls.

Rabbits may not have souls but they are highly sociable. During the autumn and early winter you could dig half a dozen grown rabbits out of the same burrow, as if they had been huddling there for warmth and companionship. As indeed they had. This was a time of complete neutrality. With their sex organs regressed and inactive during the moult, even the old, staid adults showed little aggression or territorial defence behaviour, and tolerated much visiting by their own and unrelated young rabbits seeking shelter and space to live in the warm central warrens. These visitors took over any flats and tenements left vacant by the death of previous occupants, or by burrowing birds departed overseas.

It was soon obvious to me that rabbit society is a matriarchy, revolving around the fecund doe. The buck makes a great show out of doors, but the nest and home-making is her office; and he is lost without her. His function is to keep the grazing ground inviolate for the nourishment of the family unit.

To do this in a crowded society he must subjugate all other males who by their presence challenge his dominion. This is accomplished by various forms of display. If an intruder did not retreat immediately a dominant buck might dash straight upon him, and engage in a bloody battle. In fighting each tries to bite the head and neck, and the vulnerable ear, of the other. They fall into a clinch lying face to face on one side, scramming with the front, and kicking with the long needle-like hind, claws which can penetrate the stomach wall. The fur flies. The loser screams in agony as the chisel teeth bite deep and finally the vanquished rabbit runs away, perhaps with a torn ear, or otherwise wounded, occasionally mortally.

But fighting on the whole is rarely fatal. A powerful buck can scare another away simply by displaying hostility, by walking towards the intruder with a special stiff-legged gait, tail well up on the rump and hind legs not lowered as in the normal hopping walk, in fact much like a dog making itself larger than life in order to impress a rival before attacking it. Aggressive intentions can also be signalled by various displacement actions which relieve tension, such as grazing more rapidly than usual – nibbling the grass furiously while approaching and eyeing the stranger; or digging a scrape in the ground with flying forepaws.

Rabbits are probably colour-blind, like most nocturnal or crepuscular animals. They see well, but recognition of each other is principally by scent, since they have virtually no language beyond a rare grunt, and the scream of distress. You could watch the ever-twitching nostrils exploring the air as each rabbit emerged from the burrow and read the many olfactory signs of individual activity in the colony.

A mature buck in breeding condition has a stronger smell than the doe, even to the weak human nose. A dominant male marks out the limits of his grazing territory by depositing pellets and urine along its boundary. He will squirt urine, by a flick of his hindquarters sideways, upon any conspicuous object within the territory, even occasionally upon another rabbit (but not, I am pleased to add, upon his mate!). During the breeding season a secretion from the anal glands gives the faecal pellets a characteristically powerful odour. Another gland, the sebaceous gland under the chin, is more strongly developed in the buck than the doe; the scented exudation from this gland causes the fur there to become matted into a kind of beard. The adult male further advertises his presence on his home territory by brushing his chin frequently on the ground, an action which releases droplets of scent. He may sometimes stroke his mate with his chin, and thus label her indubitably as his property, by means of this unmistakable olfactory badge.

In spite of the popular belief that rabbits are extremely promiscuous, the behaviour of our marked individuals suggested the contrary. The buck was almost uxorious in his loving attention to his mate, frequently licking and washing her face, and sitting beside her, especially on fine calm afternoons with no wind. It was a pretty sight when the pair lay stretched out together, white flanks exposed to the warmth of the sun, and perhaps with one or two of their kittens playing, or resting alongside.

The buck showed no fondness for his children, but on the other hand he did not drive the little ones away if they pushed between him and their mother in search of milk or companionship. He tolerated them so long as they were small, and until his sons were old enough to challenge him. But on the island this did not happen until one or more years had passed. His sons could grow up in the same warren with his daughters; and long familiarity with both permitted their relations to remain harmonious, but only so long as the juniors remained subordinate, and never attempted to get in Papa's way. Papa was a kind of feudal lord or king in his own warren, albeit Mama – in vulgar parlance – held the purse-strings or wore the trousers. Had not Mama dug and furnished the burrow? (Papa took no real part in this.) Was she not always at home when Papa wanted her? She was a house-proud female, with no desire to wander or philander (I have seen her repulse the surreptitious attentions of the occasional male intruder).

Mama deserved to be rewarded with all the attention Papa could give. In the breeding season she was freely ready to satisfy the sexual needs of Papa. As a result she conceived once a month regularly, mating shortly after each parturition, and at intervals also during pregnancy. For a few months in early spring she was in truth very much a hard-worked married woman. To support her pregnancies she had an enormous appetite, and spent much time in grazing, with few moments left over for fun and games. She could be irritable, even to boxing her mate's ears with scrabbling forepaws at times; and she drove away other does if they came too near, with the same display of forepaws.

She had a serious problem with the arrival of the shear-waters and puffins in the spring. Usually she had by then safely deposited her first litter of the season deep in some cul-de-sac in the burrow-system, and the kittens might be old enough to take care of themselves. But often I would find a home-hunting shearwater or puffin had burst into the nest of a rabbit, and pulled it to pieces. The second litter would have to be deposited elsewhere.

In nest-making the doe scratches out a suitable recess into which she first carries a mass of dry grass. She next burrows into this pile to make a hollow. Just before parturition she strips most of the soft fur from her belly, thus exposing her teats (usually eight in number), and lines the hollow with this warm material. All these actions of course take place in dark-ness. The young, between two and six in number on Skok-holm (but larger litters are more usual on the mainland) need this warmth, since they are born hairless, blind and deaf. The doe licks and cleans them at once, at the same time eating the foetal placenta, and so severing the umbilical cord. She remains to suckle them for several hours, and until they have settled down. She then goes forth to graze, but before leaving the burrow she pushes a thick plug of earth over the top of the nest, concealing it and incidentally shutting out the free circulation of air. But no matter: the tiny morsels of life thrive without it. The doe returns once, or rarely twice, in each twenty-four hours to suckle and clean her babies (she swal-lows their milky faeces). By the end of the first week their eyes and ears are open, and the downy fur is growing. They begin to push through the plug of the airless nest about the tenth day. They are able to run to the burrow mouth and start to nibble grass when three weeks of age.

Before they are a month old the doe, if she is pregnant

again, loses interest in them – not surprisingly – as she prepares a new nest for the next family. But if she is not pregnant she will continue to suckle for several days longer – so long as her milk is still flowing.

But how did we know all this? Some of this maternal, and much other behaviour, we observed underground by making an artificial burrow in a mound of earth placed against a plate glass window forming one side of a wooden hut. Inside the hut we could sit in comfort, quietly, hidden by a screen, and study the rabbits sitting in the artificial recesses and passages (re-inforced with concrete to prevent burrowing) we had made for them on the other side of the glass. The artificial 'viewing' burrows were connected with an enclosed plot of grazing, and the rabbits, although they could not escape altogether, could come and go and feed at will. They behaved naturally, going out at noon and at night to graze. When at home at other times they rested, doing little or nothing. But this inaction was natural and important. The rabbits were sleeping off the effects of the activity out of doors, and digesting the food taken during the hours of grazing.

I particularly wanted to study the rabbits' curious method of 'chewing the cud'. It was difficult to observe this in the open. The Bible (*Leviticus*, 11) lays down that the cony shall not be eaten because it 'cheweth the cud' and is therefore unclean; but until recently the significance of this old Jewish law was overlooked or little understood by students of the rabbit. In our artificial underground warren we could watch the process closely, and its importance quickly became obvious.

It could easily be overlooked. There would be a swift bending of the head during which the rabbit's long ears almost touched the ground as its mouth was pushed between its hind legs. The head in fact quite masked the operation for the observer; it seemed to be only a preening action, but was immediately followed by a mouthing and swallowing of an unseen object. Chewing the cud in this manner may seem a disgusting habit, and when in 1940 Dr E. L. Taylor of Weybridge showed that re-ingestion of faecal pellets also occurred in the domestic rabbit, a fellow scientist Thomas Hare wrote in the *Veterinary Record* in the same year that he thought it must be a depraved appetite, or pica; and he rhymed:

E.L.T. is very funny
In stating that a normal bunny
Enjoying health and merriment
Always eats its excrement.
To claim this for the Weybridge rabbits
Does not surprise us, since their habits
Must conform with expectations
And Civil Service Regulations.

Recently other workers have proved that the habit is hardly a vicious or depraved one. The remarkable fact is that the pellets which the rabbit takes direct from the anus are soft, and rich in bacteria, phosphorus, sodium, potassium and lactic acid, which aid digestion in much the same way as chewing the semi-digested cud does in cattle, sheep and other ruminants. These soft pellets differ very much from the normal hard pellets which rabbits drop in the open, and which are composed of tough indigestible plant remains with all nutritive value extracted. In re-ingesting these soft pellets the rabbit is performing a doubly economical operation of keeping its underground home in a clean and sanitary condition, while enjoying a vitamin-rich snack which is necessary to the proper digestion of its bulky vegetable diet!

Our observation of the rabbit below ground showed that the soft pellets appear several hours after the night's grazing, on a full stomach. They are taken direct from the anus and swallowed whole; therefore, strictly speaking, the rabbit does not chew the cud. It has been shown that these pellets pass down the gullet whole and remain for about six hours 'incubating' in the upper part of the stomach on top of the mass of recently ingested grass and vegetable matter. They finally dissolve, yielding their rich contents of active bacteria and lactic acid to assist the break-down of the coarse food and roughage.

We never saw a rabbit pass a pellet, nor did it urinate, below ground. But as soon as it emerges in the afternoon it begins to evacuate the characteristic hard pellets, and probably the physical activity of grazing and other employment outdoors encourages defaecation. Meanwhile new soft pellets form in the blind gut below the stomach, from the secretions of the caecum. While the rabbit is grazing, re-filling the stomach and skipping about, and when it returns to rest in the burrow later, these soft pellets pass gradually down the lower intestine in glossy sticky clusters resembling small liquorice balls. They cling to the anus, and may be a source of mild irritation, inducing the rabbit to clean them away, and swallow them whole – and evidently with relish.

Re-ingestion may be a lowly subject to discuss; but is obviously an advantageous habit, procuring sanitation of the burrow, providing food enjoyed in idle hours, and improving digestion. It perhaps helps to explain why rabbits are capable of remaining below a long time without obvious starvation when there is danger from traps and other predatory activity outside; also, it is said, when their burrows are covered with snow, they remain in good condition for days without grazing. But as to the last we had no opportunity to study conditions under snow, which is rare and never lies long on our western coast.

As seen in the artificial burrow the family made a pleasant domestic picture at moments when the kittens were old enough to leave the nest and cuddle together with their parents. We grew very attached to the number-tagged individuals as we watched them for many hours underground; we gave them proper names. But they were of course unnaturally protected from outside interference by the fence I had put around their grazing ground to prevent them from leaving the experimental area. The doe wild and free on the island, as I have already said, had a serious problem if the shearwaters and puffins occupied her burrow. This was obvious when we inserted a puffin momentarily into the artificial warren; we watched the bewildered bird attack and with its powerful bill put to flight the rabbits it bumped into underground.

For her second nest the island doe might not be able to use a corner in her own warren because of this interference from birds. If not she dug a fresh, shallow burrow in the open. She would work with surprising speed, disappearing below the surface within an hour or two. Next day the new burrow might be complete, and smoothed over with earth so cleverly and neatly, level with the surface, that unless I had carefully noted its position it could easily be overlooked. Nevertheless it was more vulnerable to predation than a nest deep underground.

It is the fate of the younger subordinate breeding does of a rabbit community to have to make a 'stop' (as we called these outdoor nests) in this way for their first litters. The dominant doe (we called her the queen), in her warren, naturally occupied the best nest site at home; and she would not tolerate even her own daughters inspecting her nursery.

The single doe (Miriam) in my Extensive Pen of one acre, enjoying unlimited food, bred early and late, and each time produced large litters (which we removed, except for one daughter (Sheba) whom we allowed to remain: and she too produced large families). By contrast, in the Intensive Acre, as the numbers of rabbits reached a peak of population of some 24 adult does over the four years, they produced fewer litters, of smaller size, and later in the spring. Their overcrowding represented conditions over the whole island at the end of each summer; but we had the advantage of being able to mark and study as individuals the inhabitants of our enclosures.

In the first year of observation of the Intensive Acre, two bucks, out of six pairs of rabbits introduced to form the nucleus, dominated half an acre each, and occupied the best burrows, each with his chosen queen. The four secondary bucks, unable to escape far, took up territory within that of the two king bucks. The kings secured dominance, as in the wild free state, by constantly patrolling, and a display of readiness to fight. But generally fighting was avoided, by the secondary individuals retiring in good time. Thus an ordered society was maintained for long periods by the strongest male, who was usually the oldest buck. Dominance, as in human society, depended in the main on seniority and the experience which accompanies age; and once kingship was established the peck-order was maintained as a habit during that breeding season. The youngest were at the bottom of the order.

The queen was sedentary, and around her warren was centred the general activity of each group, composed of the king, their progeny, and older children or other individuals submissive or powerful enough to retain a position there. Naturally the dominant pair enjoyed the best sleeping berths in the royal warren, in which the queen had her litters (exclusively in the Intensive Pen), but secondary females – as I have said –

were usually obliged to nest in stops dug in the open. When the progeny of these outsiders left the stop and attempted to invade the royal warren in the breeding season they were driven away by the king or queen. Thus the children of the royal pair enjoyed a social advantage over rabbits born outside the central warren, and were more likely to succeed to dominant positions as they grew up. They were aristocrats with better accommodation, better protection, and the best grazing available, at least during childhood and adolescence.

This became more and more important as overcrowding increased, causing psychological tension, and inhibiting successful breeding, first among the secondary does, and later affecting the fecundity of the dominant females. There was increasing strife between bucks. The king had difficulty in controlling his rivals. The grazing area contained in the Intensive Acre was carved out into smaller kingdoms. There was physical stress, too, due to undernourishment as the pasture deteriorated through overgrazing, and the palatable plants disappeared. The Pen was becoming a slum. And disease, especially coccidiosis, was taking a severe toll.

In the first breeding season in this Pen there had been 100 per cent increase of population; but in the fourth year less than 20 per cent. It was time to release the rabbits from further suffering, but it had been a valuable experiment, explaining to us what could happen (and indeed did happen only one year later) to the rabbits free and uncontrolled at Skokholm. Had we allowed the Intensive Acre to continue to exist with its peak population of around fifty adults in 1958, there could have been the same severe crash of population which happened at Skokholm in the winter of 1959–60. The overcrowded island rabbits died in thousands: from a possible maximum of 10,000 they fell to below 240. Such a calamitous decline had never happened before in the history of the rabbits as we knew it; it was an example of what overpopulation can do once the standard of living declines, followed by undernourishment and epidemic disease – in this instance virulent coccidiosis (myxomatosis as an epidemic at Skokholm without the rabbit flea being virtually impossible).

In effect the Skokholm rabbits had suddenly declined, from around forty, to one per acre. The sequel was interesting. The pasture did not recover until midsummer, but was then so plentiful that the surviving does came into breeding condition in September and October, an unprecedented event on Skokholm, for autumn is the season of complete rest from breeding when the male gonads are normally regressed and inactive. Each doe had one litter then, and breeding continued on a high level of fertility – exactly as in my Extensive Pen – while the grazing was so good.

Normally the Skokholm doe, under average conditions of climax population or near it, has no more than two litters of two to four or five kittens each spring. She may mate early and often, but there is not enough food both to feed her and support a pregnancy until the first flush of grass in April. Under the conditions of stress already described, provided the buck is fertile, a doe may conceive after mating, but she has an interesting form of birth-control. She is able to re-absorb one or more or all of the growing embryos during a pregnancy, if exterior conditions are unfavourable for rearing the young. Such re-absorbing (resorption) takes place very rapidly, generally about half-way through or later in the four weeks of the gestation period. The embryos die and shrivel away, and the embryonic and placental tissues are resorbed into the maternal system, without abortion. Milk appears in the mammary glands and, if all the embryos have died, the doe comes into oestrus and mates as if live birth had occurred. We do not yet know what the chemical nature of this form of birth-control is. We only know that the rabbit has a self-regulating fecundity mechanism which is triggered by these density factors, that is, by the degree of stress and tension in competition for food and shelter.

It will be seen from all these researches that the mechanism of reproduction and of social behaviour in the wild rabbit is flexibly adapted to the opportunities for expansion, as well as to the pressures leading to stability, of population numbers. But the rabbit has so far kept secret the mechanism, so valuable if only it could be applied to the control of human populations, by which an undesirable pregnancy is disposed of, so discreetly and without abortion.

Perhaps man should pay more attention to this aspect of rabbit physiology and try to find the chemical formula by which he may avert the final catastrophe (which swept away 98 per cent of the unthinking Skokholm rabbits) of overpopulation, malnutrition, disease and death? For with this key to birth-control man, with his thinking brain, should do better than the rabbits. He should be able to realize his hope of a richer, better world of fewer people, with room for wild animals and plants and trees too; and save the earth from becoming an ant-heap, and from the diseases of overpopulation – genocide and war.

9 Guillemots

First of the sea-birds to return are the gregarious, penguin-like, noisy guillemots. A few of them scarcely depart from the seaway around Skokholm all winter. In the autumn these auks moult into a whiter plumage, losing the black collar of summer, and look so different that the fishermen used to tell us that they were not the same birds as the 'eligugs' (local name for guillemots, and derived from the call of the bird). They knew the winter-plumaged guillemot by the name 'herring-bird' because it was seen at the only time the fishermen went out to fish in winter, in the few calm days when it was possible to anchor the herring-nets to intercept the spawning shoals in the bays.

The birds are seeking the half-grown fry of fishes on which the herrings themselves are feeding. I would see them swimming below the screaming flocks of gulls hovering and dipping upon the swift tideways. But the fully adult guillemots and razorbills put on their black collars again before the turn of the year, while the immature birds lingered in the 'herring-bird' plumage.

It was delightful to encounter, on some fine mornings in late December, the guillemots suddenly gathered in hundreds close under the island cliffs, perhaps with a few razorbills among them. As the sun rose more and more birds flew in to join the assembly. Presently they would begin joyous flights along the cliffs, preparatory to landing on the breeding ledges. This land-coming so early in the winter is expressed in a local belief that the eligugs always come home for the Christmas celebrations.

Watching these first arrivals it was plain to me that the birds were in fine breeding plumage and high spirits. The incessant murmuration of groaning calls was evocative of the sea-bird summer, despite the often bitter winter wind. The assembled auks performed their fascinating water-dances, as communal and excitatory as any jungle dance indulged by equatorial bush peoples. A party of a dozen or so birds would form two lines facing, about one yard apart – not with any exactness, but roughly so – as in the human song-dance of 'Nuts in May'. As they paddled towards each other or were washed closer by the movement of the restless waves, they became more excited, groaning and fencing the air with their bills. When collision seemed imminent the whole party dived simultaneously, an action which seemed to release tension, and the birds chased each other under the water exuberantly, with swift paddling movements of the half-closed wings. Soon they would surface, once more to reform their lines, then again to dive simultaneously. And so the water play lasted for an hour or two, interrupted with joy-flights to the ledges.

There is no mating so early in the season. It is a near-sexless display of *joie de vivre*, a midwinter reunion of the auk clans after the five months of the moulting and wandering period, an annual general meeting or party, with committees holding discussions on the familiar cliff terraces. The old hands are busy checking on their favourite territories on those land ledges where in five months' time they will lay the huge single, handsomely marked egg.

These midwinter assemblies are brief, just a few hours early on a sunny morning, and are over, all birds departed, by midday. The second visit might not be for several days, perhaps weeks. But how the meetings are arranged and by what signal hundreds assemble at a given hour no man yet knows. Why indeed this sudden descent upon the breeding grounds so far ahead of egg-laying? Even the gannets on the neighbouring islet of Grassholm, like the shearwaters at Skokholm, do not return until February, and they begin laying in April, well in advance of the guillemots. But there may be wisdom, both innate and learned, in this early visit by adults staking their claims to a nest site in a species so communal as the guillemot, for there is severe competition for the nest positions on the ledges. The guillemot often appears to behave in a remarkably stupid way – for instance in placing its egg in such a dangerous situation – and yet we shall see that there are several aspects of its life ashore which suggest intelligent reaction to the problems of egg and chick management.

The huge colonies on the cliffs of Skomer opposite Skokholm, but two or three miles distant, were the first to be occupied. Often the smaller cliff breeding sites on my island were not visited until February, but I had no means of knowing if Skokholm guillemots joined in the December or January parliaments at Skomer. The excitement created by gatherings of a communal species early in the season have value in stimulating pair formation and synchronizing breeding condition, resulting in earlier nesting and more successful rearing of young. In theory also there is better protection against predators, especially of the inner core of established breeders; it is the outlying individuals and smaller peripheral colonies that are most vulnerable to attack.

On first settling on the ledges the birds are nervous. They sit on the edge with their tails in space, facing the cliff wall, bowing and uttering their typical groaning calls which can be rendered as a loud grating 'murre' (hence the name in America) with a long rolling of the 'r's. Each bird is a full body length apart, for as yet the safety distance, or fear barrier of their winter life, has not been breached. It does not disappear until nearer the hour of continuous occupation in April. The initial shyness or fear of attack gradually dies away as neighbours become accustomed to the voice and presence of each other, and the pressure for breeding space increases. Meanwhile tension continues to be relieved by the incessant bowing and obeisances, fencing of the bill in the air, the mouth open to show the brilliant yellow inside, and by growling. The last is contagious, and often a whole ledgeful will make a chorus of it. The general behaviour and volume of sound somewhat resembles that of a cocktail party of men and women in black and white dress, waving their arms about and talking their heads off, with no one able to hear anything clearly except the conversation of the nearest neighbour. Argument seems to be non-stop, but actual serious disputes rare. In fighting the opponents lock bills together, and as a rule only separate as they tumble over the edge in their excitement.

Late in April the distance between male and female is at last bridged by mutual preening actions, and the pair sit side by side. If the female leaves the ledge at this intimate stage, the male sometimes follows her, and they may meet and mate on the surface of the sea below. But as a rule one of the pair retains possession of the site, or quickly returns, calling and bowing vigorously until the other joins it. Copulation is most often seen on the site where, a week or two later, the egg is laid.

My observations showed that the common guillemot, in banding studies at Skokholm, was the most communal of seabirds in respect of sharing mate, egg or chick. Other observers have also recorded this promiscuity, which has its advantages if one or other parent is absent from the crowded ledges at a critical moment, or dies. Thus in the temporary absence of her banded mate, an unbanded male was permitted to copulate with a banded female. In mating the female lies with her breast on the ledge, her tail elevated, while the male maintains his position by whirring his wings, puffin-wise. She turns her head backwards, her yellow mouth open wide and giving forth a distinctive hoarse groan of ecstacy, which can be heard at some distance.

If one moves gently, slowly, it is fairly easy to angle for and catch adult birds at the ledges with the long puffin rod tipped with a little crook for slipping over the leg. I spent many hours watching banded individuals in a small colony of two dozen pairs crowded upon the Eligug Wall on Skokholm's north cliffs. Here, in May and June, there was Standing Room Only. When all the adults were present they sat almost shoulder to shoulder. There was no room for the occasional visitor, even at times for the legitimate owner of egg or chick. Returning birds might fail to find room to alight and regain possession of their property. They would fall off in the attempt unless – at a risk of stabbing by ill-mannered occupants – they could crash-land and displace a bird in possession of the coveted spot.

There was never a lack of a willing mate, aunt, uncle, or other individual to take over the duty of incubating the egg, or brooding or feeding the chick.

When unable to gain standing room on the nursery ledge, the adult would drop down to the sea, or else alight nearby on a wider ledge or broad rock unused for breeding. This was the permanent loitering ground for off-duty and uncommitted birds. In fine, calm weather many guillemots, razorbills and puffins swim to the nearest rocks below the cliffs, and as the tide falls they scramble ashore to bask in the sun, and rest and converse by sign and voice.

All is usually quiet at night in the loomeries of the guillemots during the incubation period, for they are diurnal birds while ashore.

The pyriform shape of the egg minimizes the considerable danger of rolling over the cliff, but many eggs are lost in this way. Tests I made on the level surface of a tray showed that when the egg is fresh, with a small air space at the big end, it will roll in a tight circle if the tray is slightly tilted. But as the air space increases with incubation, the centre of gravity moves towards the small end and then the egg on the tray rolls in an even narrower circle.

This is a useful adaptation to the rolling danger: the guillemot will not lay again if its first egg has been incubated many days; but if the egg is fresh when lost another (and, if the second egg is also lost immediately, sometimes a third) will be laid in the same summer. About one-third of the first eggs to be laid are lost from various causes; one of which is human approach causing the breeding bird to fly suddenly from the ledge before it has time to disengage the egg from the brood patch.

In colour the huge handsome egg varies enormously: usually it is pale blue-green or light green, with dark brown spots, blotches and scribblings. Thus each is as distinctively marked as a human thumbprint, only more so – and far more beautiful. Experiments have shown that the female does recognize her egg among others near, on the same ledge, but if hers disappears she will willingly pirate another egg if permitted. Eggs soon become dirty from the debris and guano of the ledge, and some become completely coated with muck, which incidentally further prevents them rolling easily. In wet weather some eggs actually become stuck by guano immovably to the ledge, and so fail to hatch, since they cannot be turned. Other eggs roll into crevices from which all attempts by the owners fail to extricate them. Thus birds which choose poor sites for incubation fail to rear their posterity, and nature's selection is all in favour of the use of proper sites by the most efficient individuals.

Male and female guillemots incubate in turns: before the egg is laid each develops a large single brood patch below the breast, the bare skin and surrounding feathers of which envelop the top of the egg completely. The brooding adult shuffles its broad webbed feet under the egg so that it is not in contact with the cold rock during incubation. Thus 'carried' between feet and breast, the efficient parent can move its egg, if it has been left in a dangerous position on the ledge at the changing of the guard or through barging by neighbours, to a safer position. The anxiety of the brooding adult over its egg is pleasingly obvious.

This anxiety extends to the new-born chick when it hatches after an average of thirty-three days' incubation. Both guillemot and razorbill chicks are covered with a dark down which provides warmth in their exposed situation. They grow with astonishing rapidity, but need the warmth of the bare skin of the brood cavity of the parent for the first week. One adult stays on guard while the other forages at sea, turn and turn about. There is no time for loitering, although, interestingly enough, on return from the fishing expedition the parent does loiter and delay beside the chick, holding the fish lengthwise in its long bill for up to an hour before delivering it into the young gullet. There is a good reason for this, but how can we know if the adult is conscious of it?

The long pointed bill of the guillemot is adapted to catching whole fish a good deal larger than those taken by the thicker, shorter bill of puffin and razorbill, which bring in several small fish together, held in the bill crosswise; these small fish are fed raw and quite undigested. The comparatively large single fish brought home by the guillemot hangs with its tail protruding from the tip of the adult bill, but the spiny head is far down the gullet. As if conscious that a fresh whole fish would be indigestible the adult holds a large fish in this position until the head is partly digested, much softened, and even altogether missing, by the time the fish itself is passed to the chick. Even so, the baby seems to have a tough time getting down its gullet a fish which may be as long as its body, and one end perfectly raw! But at last it disappears, with many contortions and wriggling and muscular movements of the swollen stomach.

When hungry the baby guillemot utters 'willou, willou' incessantly – hence the name of willock given to it by the fishermen when it reaches the sea. In my colony of banded individuals at least three different adults responded to this hunger call and fed the same chick. There is also a charming communal effort to fence in the younger chicks and prevent them from tumbling over the edge: a row of adults sit with their tails outwards and breasts hemming the babies in against the wall of the cliff. They are watchful of passing gulls which are ever alert to snatch an egg or young chick; and with stabbing beaks drive away these predatory attempts.

Older chicks, well feathered at two weeks old, are more difficult to control: they like strolling little distances from home, sometimes huddling together and touching beaks, as if in a childish game. They are spoiled by the adults, who never drive them away, but respond as soon as a chick announces its hunger vociferously, or goes up to a newly arrived adult and pecks at the fish 'incubating' in the long bill – although the chick may have to wait a little while until the adult is ready to hand it over.

Some chicks are most precocious and ready to leave for the sea from fifteen days of age onwards, but others will complete three weeks on the ledges. In this phenomenally short period the chick, of course, has not had time to become full grown; in fact it is only half the size of the adult. Nor are its primary wing quills developed; the wings at this stage are stumpy affairs, with only the secondary flight feathers to aid it on its fluttering descent to the sea. But there again we see a natural selection operating: those chicks which developed quickest and escaped from the dangers of the cliffs earliest are the individuals with the best chance of surviving and reproducing their superior race.

The sea-going of the novice guillemots and razorbills is quite thrilling to watch. It is best seen in a large colony. It takes place over a brief period towards dusk, when the predatory gulls are sleepy and less likely to be hunting. Restless for one or two days previously, the feathered fledglings call excitedly and poise on the edge of their ledges. Usually one adult stands anxiously beside each chick; and other adults, infected with the general communal excitement of this important annual ceremony, swim on the water below, groaning loudly in response.

The willocking call rises to a crescendo as the chick suddenly leaps into the air, immediately followed by the adult consort which however renders no physical aid, despite the stories in the older bird-books of parents carrying young down by one wing. The youngster, even if it hits the rock on the way to the sea, bounces off unhurt, quite protected by its own light weight and the thick pad of its breast feathers.

On reaching the sea it is immediately surrounded by a covey of adults. Guided by its cries, they converge upon it, and seem even to make a mock attack, causing it to dive deeply. ('Now, Willy, first thing you must learn is to dive, your only hope of escape from those beastly gulls. Down you go! It's perfectly easy!') And so it is! The young bird is a perfect diver; and, like the young puffin and shearwater, is as much at home under as above the sea. But there is a considerable difference in after-care. The half-grown guillemot and razorbill still need parental attention, and they get it. The excitement of the sea-going ceremony – the first christening with salt water – is over, however, in a very few minutes. Then only one of the nearest adult witnesses leads the fledgling away to sea.

I would like to think, but I have not been able to prove, that the young bird, by its incessant calling on reaching the sea, is recognized by voice by its parents; and perhaps it also recognizes its own mother (or father?) by the familiar low growl which is the parental response to its willocking call. But which, if either, anxious parent conveys and attends it at sea is yet to be discovered.

You may hear the willocking cry far into the ocean for a month or two later – that appealing cry which compels one faithful adult to guard the young bird while it is flightless, perhaps feeding it for a while, and presumably teaching it how to live in the wilderness of salt water.

All I have written of the breeding biology of the guillemot

fits much of the scene in the colonies of the handsome black and white razorbills, of which up to a thousand pairs nest at Skokholm; but with one or two significant differences of habitat and incubation. The razorbill prefers, although not invariably (for it will lay its egg within the confines of the guillemot ledges), to nest in a safer place, often selecting a situation under a boulder, or some way inside a hole in the cliff, even inside the entrance to a cliff-top rabbit burrow. By its choice of a more secluded breeding site it is without the promiscuity of mating, and communal attention to egg and chick, described for the more gregarious guillemot. Finally, like the hole-nesting puffin, the razorbill has two brood patches – I do not know why, since it lays only one egg. There is a bare spot on each side of the breast; and when incubating the razorbill leans over the egg, which it draws close to the body, under one falling wing.

Banding hundreds of both species at Skokholm has shown that the razorbill wanders farther south than the guillemot: it penetrates the Mediterranean in winter, reaching the coast of Italy. Both species also visit all coasts of north-western Europe at that season, but the guillemot lives closer inshore. I could always see one or two in 'herring-bird' plumage, at any time of the winter on my sailings to and from Skokholm.

10 Mother Carey's Chickens

As for the beautiful little storm-petrels, they were the latest to return to the island in the spring, never earlier than the last week in April. From my bed beside the open window I would hear the first arrivals purring in their favourite chinks in the garden wall, just as the young Harrison daughters had heard them sixty years earlier.

Because of their small and fragile appearance, and absurdly light weight (only 28 grams), it seems incredible that these birds can ride out great storms at sea on their flimsy wings. But like the shearwaters they are thoroughly at home in the roughest weather. I have watched them from a storm-tossed trawler. They followed the wake churned up by the labouring propeller, diving and disappearing under the waves as they spotted small specks of food for a few seconds, before rising and fluttering along, dainty webbed feet paddling the surface with ease. By hugging the water closely they seemed to gain protection from the savage winds which made the trawler heel to leeward. The ability to walk on the surface of the water, wings aflutter, gave rise to the name – from the apostle Peter, who did so.

On land they are not quite so nocturnal as the shearwater, although with obvious reason fearing attack from the predatory gulls on the island. Whether the night is dark or fine the storm-petrels come home from sea about an hour after sunset, and leave with the first flush of dawn. But they are noisiest on the darkest nights. The bird which has spent the day in the nest begins purring even before sundown, reeling off the long continuous 'urr-rr-rr' song which ends in an abrupt hiccup –

'chikka!' A friend of mine likened the sound to 'a fairy being sick'.

The function of the song is plain – to advertise territory, a home, a desirable nesting site; and to attract a mate. And possibly the storm-petrel uses its voice to echo-locate its home, at least on the darkest nights. A male already at home indicates by this purring song where the nesting cranny is, and on clear nights the prospecting incoming female is able to find it by sight. No doubt voice recognition is important in the dark burrow, but all petrel conversations seem the same to the human ear. I never discovered whether the male has a different repertoire, but if so it must be within the same limited range of notes, not loud but with a resonant quality which carries far.

The whole behaviour of these dainty petrels is fairy-like. Ann would plead to be allowed to stay up to see the 'storm-fairies'; she had her own pet pair in the garden wall with whom she exchanged a few words now and then. In the twilight of a clear evening it is possible to see them with the naked eye, as although their bodies are soot-black the rump is pure white. As it flits past the white spot resembles a zigzagging butterfly in typical wavering flight. It must be an excellent guide to the excited birds in their aerial courtship, which is a feature of nights in May and June before the egg is laid. In these fairy chases one bird follows the other in tight circles above a nesting area; and often a third and even a fourth bird will join in. There is a soft rustle as of fairy wings as the petrels circle round, uttering at intervals a wickering noise as well as snatches of the purring and hiccuping song.

When handled at the nest the storm-petrel, like many other members of this family of tube-nosed birds, will squirt an oily fluid from the mouth, at the same time covering the large nostrils with the discharge. This has a powerful musky smell, which also clings to the bird and its burrow. It was our habit to find the nesting crevices of the 'stormies' by creeping along the hedge-walls of the home meadow on a calm evening, with nose to the stones. If we did not locate each occupied burrow by the purring song, we could always find it by the olfactory evidence.

Some nesting crevices ran deep into the walls, but on the

other hand many petrels could be seen sitting on the bare earth only a dozen inches behind an opening between the stones, and in a strong light by day. These shallow-sited nests were ideal for observing the breeding habits and recording the incubation and fledging periods, quite unknown at that time. We marked with numbered pegs a score of nests in the hedge-walls of the home meadow, where it was possible to pull out the covering stone and use it as an inspection door without destroying the site.

In addition there were hundreds of petrels nesting else-where, in every kind of – mostly inaccessible – small hole, from deep in the boulders under the cliffs, to the side-passages in shearwater burrows too small for any save the petrels to squeeze into. Today probably over a thousand pairs nest at Skokholm.

Petrels are good at squeezing. They can insert themselves through crevices barely wide enough for my two fingers to enter. Many nesting recesses are so small that the brooding bird has no room to open its wings in mating and other opera-tions. But mating has rarely been observed. Probably it takes place in the open – I twice surprised a marked pair in sugges-tive attitudes near the entrance to their crevice.

As in the shearwater there was a prolonged settling-in and courtship period between the arrival of my marked adult petrels and the laying of the single large egg. The male appears first and spends more time in the nest, evidently protecting the site from rivals and encouraging with song the female to join him in possession.

Year after year ownership of the burrow is re-established by the older, breeding petrels; and it is the same picture as with the shearwater, puffin and other species where the sexes are outwardly alike: faithfulness to the old home, despite a winter of wandering as lone independent individuals; and mutual courtship to maintain the pair-bond. Banded male and female petrels have come together at the familiar nest as long as both have lived, to re-unite in yet another season's effort to rear a child.

In the courtship period the male petrel stands watch over the nest by day more often than his mate; but the pair having established their claim early in the season, and left the pro-

149

prietory mark of their scent there, further residence by day is, on average, meagre, less than one day in four – probably because of the need to feed at sea and keep up their glossy breeding condition. There are more night visits, approximately every other night one or both birds come home for a visiting period of two or three hours during which scraping of the site for the egg takes place in rather desultory fashion, much interrupted with purring song, and doubtless mating, as the moment approaches for the egg to be laid.

Petrels easily desert the site, and even the egg, if handled too often. After losing several nests we learned to limit our visits to ascertaining which of the pair was at the nest, using a little stick to poke into the hole and lift the bird's breast gently under the light of a torch (males were banded on the right and females on the left leg). To minimize disturbance still further we devised the simple plan of placing a lattice door of matchsticks or dead bracken stems across the entrance to each occupied crevice; the petrel easily brushed these aside and so established for us whether there had been entry or exit since the last recorded observation. In this way also we found that there was much visiting by unbanded birds, and this tended to increase as more immature adults arrived in June and July.

The large egg, laid on the bare earth, is pure white, but often has a zone of faint red freckles at the large end. Both parents incubate. Unless they had been unduly disturbed for any reason during the period of incubation, we found that the egg hatched in thirty-eight to forty days. Another observer at Skokholm, Peter Davis, confirmed this incubation period – long for a bird as small as a swallow – when he had thirty-six nests under observation; and he found that the egg could stand periods of chilling lasting three days if both parents were absent. In one nest the egg was chilled for eleven days in spells (one of five days) yet managed to hatch after fifty days. Resistance of the egg to chilling occurs in the shearwater also, and must be useful to these albatross-like birds which wander far in search of food during the nesting period, in case the off-duty bird fails to relieve the sitting bird before hunger forces it to depart.

The storm-petrels share incubation by shifts of three days

(occasionally shorter, or up to five days). The bird off-duty returns well-fed, but may not always persuade its fasting mate to leave. ('No, dear-r-r, you'r-r-re not tur-r-rning me out just yet! Buzz-zz-zz off and come back tomorr-rr-ow. I don't feel hungr-rr-rr-rry, me dear-r-r-r!' One could imagine the purring conversation as one listened with ear to the nest-crevice.) They are affectionate, billing and cooing at the nest; nevertheless they do not feed each other when they meet there.

On warm midsummer nights it was pleasant to sit quietly in the bracken opposite the nesting crevices in the old walls, and study the arrivals and departures and listen to the conversations. I could put out my hand and catch a storm-petrel at that awkward second or two of folding its large wings preparatory to squeezing into the narrow entrance. This was the vulnerable moment when, on bright nights, the gulls roosting nearby might seize a petrel, tear it apart and swallow all but the tough wings.

Another predator which found the petrels easy to snatch at the moment of alighting was the little owl. This handsome bird, named after the goddess Athene, would alight on a wall near a nest hole and remain motionless until it could ambush the homing or departing petrel. When I discovered a nest of this owl in a rabbit burrow, at the back of which over a hundred headless corpses of petrels had been stored away – a larder for a rainy day that never came, for petrels were so easy to catch fresh every night – I captured and deported the owls. They were banded and sent 180 miles by car to Bath, from which salubrious neighbourhood they never returned.

In future it became necessary to exile or shoot all little owls as fast as they arrived on Skokholm – a procedure adopted with less regret than might be supposed, since this owl is not a true native of Britain, but was introduced late in the last century. (It spread rapidly and reached this coast in numbers by the 1920s, acquiring notoriety for its appetite for small birds; but it has since settled down to exist in much smaller numbers adjusted to a food supply which includes beetles, worms and other small items – in fact it is a respectable citizen on the mainland today, but must needs be banished from the storm-petrel nesting grounds.)

Control of the largest gull, the great black-back, is also

carried out regularly at Skokholm today, with beneficial results for the petrels and many smaller sea-birds upon which it preys so heavily all summer.

The petrel chick emerges from the egg by breaking the shell around the large end with the tiny sharp pickaxe of the egg-tooth on top front of the beak – a weapon which presently drops off as the bird grows. The nestling is covered with a silvery-grey down, but the head has a curious large bald spot. At birth the eyes are closed and the head drops to the ground in a helpless attitude. The parent on duty guards it day and night for the first week, by which time the eyes are open and the head erect. In the second week the parents leave it alone by day; and both now collect food to satisfy its growing appetite. The second down pushes out the first until the chick – like the shearwater child – resembles a ball of greyish-brown wool. At five weeks the feathers are well developed and the coat of warm down is gradually moulted.

If the adult is caught as it enters the nest it may vomit the contents of its crop, consisting of an oily mess of tiny fish remains, which is normally pumped into the chick in the same controlled fashion as the shearwater baby is fed. Peter Davis found that the weight of food delivered in one feed by a parent did not vary much above 6 grams; so if both parents fed it the same night it almost doubled its own weight in a couple of hours. On rare occasions when one or both parents died during the fledging period, the chick showed a remarkable ability to survive a long time on less or no food, an adaptation useful in a species with a protracted breeding season. When starved thus the nestlings of such species as albatross, shearwater, petrel and swift seem able to resist death by a slowing down of the metabolism, that is, by reduction of heart-beat and temperature – as in the hibernating mammal. After days without food the young petrel or shearwater at Skokholm feels cold and half-dead to the hand, reminding me of the rigid, almost moribund, condition of the humming-birds I examined at a zoo one night, for these tiny birds also resist death by starvation in this way – if they kept up their high day temperature without feeding over the long darkness of night, the loss of energy from their tiny bodies would be disastrous. (Large birds, such as eagles and ostriches, can suffer much longer fasts, because there is less loss of heat-energy from a surface small in relation to the large bulk of the body.)

A well-fed petrel chick fattens visibly up to the fiftieth day, after which there is a sharp decline. The parents have lost interest quite suddenly; probably because of their need to moult their worn plumage far at sea.

The abandoned chick, still downy but with the wing-quills grown, remains where it was born for the next few days alone – matchsticks placed in the nest entrance once more proved this. Then, like the deserted shearwater fledgling, it emerges for a while each night to exercise its wings. It is full grown, as large and heavy as an adult. But it is comparatively nimble on the wing, and about the sixty-second day of its life it scrambles to the nearest high point – the top of a wall or an outcrop of rock, and flies away to sea, to face the approach of winter and great storms quite alone.

I have taken fledgling petrels at this abandoned stage – in October and November – direct from their crevice, and although they have never flown before, and possibly never fully exercised their wings, when released over the sea each one has shown an eagerness not to touch the water. As long as I have been able to watch it the tiny two-months-old fledgling has continued on its graceful zigzag flight away out to sea, keeping low over the waves.

A marvellous, humbling, sight.

L'Envoi

The years were flying by. When war broke out in 1939, we had just re-established sheep on the island, following the success of the rabbit gassing experiment. I still had the mountain stallion Sugarback to ride. Ann was nine years old, away at boarding school, but she was home for the holidays, when her principal joy was to ride her own pony, Judy, a wife I had obtained for Sugarback. Both were bay ponies, free-born in the Presely Mountains which lie on the misty horizon far to the north-east of Skokholm.

A high-spirited pony stallion is quite a handful to control, especially when he prefers not to be ridden, and is cunning to swell his girth when being saddled, in the hope that the saddle will loosen and fall off, rider and all. But Sugarback was sure-footed, his bold glance darting now ahead and now underfoot to the rough ground as he galloped over the bluebells and the cushions of sea-pinks, noting the bird and rabbit holes. If he stumbled with one foot in a burrow he recovered without throwing my twelve stone overboard. He was quite used to puffins and rabbits leaping forth from beneath his feet.

He was named Sugarback, said Ann (then very small and the only human child on the island), 'Because when I give him a lump of sugar, he simply takes it from your hand and drops it back again.'

Sugarback and his wife Judy settled down happily to the simple life on the free range of Skokholm's 240 acres. The salt-sweetened pasture was fattening after their thin mountain diet. They ate the long bog-grass which the rabbits disliked. Judy produced three foals in as many years: Petronella, Lollipop and Arabella were first favourites among the animal companions of Ann, who had a vivid imagination which kept her from feeling lonely. The goats were next on her list of young friends she could talk with, and even give them lessons as she milked them. Sugarback would look in at milking time, twice daily; afterwards he would tease and chase the goats – his idea of horse-play. Out of his fondness for Ann, who petted him, he may have been jealous of them.

Sugarback was useful to drag driftwood baulks out of the sea and up the cliffs, and to draw the little cart piled high with hay, or a load of peat from the turbary. He also earned his keep by pulling the trams along the mile-long light railway between the landing place and the lighthouse, bringing oil, coal and stores from the quay, and water from our well, for the lighthouse keepers. For this service I was paid by the lighthouse authority, Trinity House. He looked handsome in his set of shining Swansea harness.

Judy was a good deal more sedate than her husband, and carried Ann at a gentler pace. Her eldest foal Petronella was broken to ride by Ann, by constant handling since birth – a young-love affair of mutual devotion. Ann claimed that Petronella had a poetic, dreamy nature – she always listened to rhymes with her head on one side.

When war broke out we had to evacuate the island on notice from the War Office, which intended to fortify Skokholm (fortunately they did not do so in the end) because of the island's position commanding the seaward approaches to Milford Haven, which became an Atlantic convoy assembly base. We had to transport 100 sheep, the goats, and Judy and her three fillies to the mainland. Sugarback still had his official transport duties to perform and had to remain. It was a miserable and memorable occasion when he watched the undignified departure of his four mares haltered and docile under nets. As the over-loaded *Storm-Petrel* moved out of the red rocks of the island haven he pawed the ground and ran wildly along the top of the cliffs, neighing his distress, his fine mane and long tail floating high in the air.

In 1946 the island was re-occupied as a bird observatory, but by then the deportees were dispersed over the face of Britain (at least two of Judy's grandchildren are reported doing well in English shires). When I went up to salute Sugarback on my return to Skokholm he eyed me with a distinct coolness; it was uncertain what memories he was harbouring. At any rate my first attempt to ride him after several years was defeated. I was tumbled suddenly into the bluebells, by his old trick of deflating his belly, and swerving to slip the saddle.

The lighthouse authority now decided to modernize the island transport. Not that Sugarback had failed to give satisfaction – he was still in his prime. He could pull with perfect ease two trams holding four 40-gallon barrels of oil – well over half a ton without the weight of the trams – along the rails. But the engineers believed that a three-wheeler motor tractor would be more docile and just as efficient. The tramlines were upheaved and thrown aside. The tractor skidded and slipped on the greasy roadway and failed to carry more than one barrel at a time – but that is another story. Trinity House might have felt thwarted by the inefficiency of their new up-to-date transport; but they rightly harboured no unkind feelings about their late equine servant, and courteously offered to bring him ashore to be of use to me in mainland spheres, where perhaps he would see once more some of his own kind. Undoubtedly he had been lonely.

I agreed to this, because Sugarback, out of that loneliness and his natural inquisitiveness, had caused some trouble to the bird-watchers and other students of wild life at the reopened observatory, by seeking their company and poking nose and hoof into delicate experimental machinery, watch-tents and observation blinds. Thrice did the lighthouse relief ship anchor off Skokholm and put a launch ashore to collect Sugarback; but embarking a spirited stallion on slippery landing steps proved impossible. Did he remember the abduction of his mares from this very spot? Or was there after all a conspiracy to keep him in the island? Certainly there were sighs of relief when Sugarback kicked and plunged his way back to freedom.

In spite of his habit of joining in the outdoor activities, from puffin-catching to picnicking, even nosing his way into the house, most people learned to love him. He was a strong character and a shrewd natural watcher of the nature-watchers.

He knew when anyone was sympathetic towards him, or hostile or afraid, and he behaved accordingly.

The extradition order was never carried out. For ten more years of fruitful observation of wild life by many visitors, Sugarback remained, an interested spectator, a familiar inhabitant, idle and growing old gracefully with flowing mane, and tail sweeping the ground. His warm bay coat was turning grey. Yes, surely he was old now, twenty-five years at least, perhaps even thirty? And old ponies must die.

Coming through his last winter in fine thick coat, he was observed to be more than usually quiet and friendly to all who spoke to him when the observatory was re-opened in the spring. It was almost as if he was saying his goodbyes. He no longer galloped. He teased and nipped people no more. He allowed the goats to graze around him, as if glad of their company. He was calm at last.

He continued his habit of grazing slowly across the island from one favourite standing place to another, punctually visiting the lighthouse kitchen in the west, and the observatory refectory – the Wheelhouse – in the east, for the tit-bits which the cooks never failed to provide when he tapped and pushed against the door. South Crags was a nook he much liked to shelter in, taking no heed of the screams of the gulls nesting in the bracken there. He often waded into the shallow North Pond and sipped a drink, then stood a long time four-square in the centre, his fetlocks cooled by the rippling water, his tail whipping over the surface.

One bright May day he remained standing so long in the pond that his human friends grew alarmed. At that time young Dido was cook, whom he knew well from profitable exchanges at the Wheelhouse door. She waded to him, and tried to persuade him to move, lifting one wet leg after another for him. But he did not stir. He laid his cheek to hers, as often she had taught him to do. She spoke quietly to him – and there were tears streaming from her eyes. He was just tired out, she thought; not in pain, but with the heart beating too slow. She groomed and coaxed him.

He remained perfectly upright and very still. When she moved away he whinnied, but would not follow her. She fetched an apple and a bucket of fresh spring water, but he refused these refreshments he used to enjoy so much. The students and other island inhabitants were gathering around the pond, for it was felt that the end was near.

Dido called him to follow her. He whinnied once more, but only looked around him, quietly. Then at last he made a great effort, as if to please his friends. He walked slowly to the foot of the South Crags. He lay down, folding his knees stiffly.

He died peacefully in his sleep that night. But his name lives still – on the map. His favourite standing place, where he was buried with reasonable ceremony for a horse, and a stone erected, is known as Sugar's Delight.

*

With the passing of Sugarback, the old order of island life finally disappeared. All things change and die, and are reborn. After the war we did not return to live, but only occasionally to stay, on the island. But, like those of the shearwaters and puffins, new generations of human inhabitants were to supplant the old. There was a steady procession of other, younger observers and lovers of the Crusoe life anxious to continue the work we had begun; to set up each spring the migratory bird traps, blown down in winter gales; to maintain the observations on banded resident birds, on the shifting populations of the rabbits; even to research expensively on the house-mouse which, said to have arrived about 1903 in a load of straw used to bed down a colt conveyed to Skokholm in a boat from the mainland, has increased and occupied every corner of the island in the absence of competition from other mice. There are many advantages, and a useful limitation territorially, in research on all forms of life upon a moderately small island, now fitted with modern amenities and conveniences, far from the bustle of cities and the haunts of men.

Ornithologists, mammalogists, botanists, ecologists: before me on my desk are some of the results of that research – a shelf loaded with new information published in scientific journals and reports, on almost every biological subject of field research you could think of, from the higher animals and the birds, to plant life, pond water life, butterflies, moths, ants, spiders, harvestmen, beetles, down to such lowly organisms as the fleas and flatflies and other parasites; even the basidiomycetes (fungi) of Sugarback's dung (a surprising number of species recorded, with interesting if jaw-breaking scientific names) have been studied. Let me add here how grateful I am to the authors of these articles, for their work has enabled me to round off some of my own early observations, and they have helped to solve some of the problems of island ecology that puzzled me.

My space is running out. I had intended to bring into this book much more of the story of the other chief companions of my life on Skokholm. I have hardly begun to describe the habits of those magnificent flying machines forever circling and calling overhead: the gulls; or of the oystercatchers, those amusing, wary friends which each day greeted me by every outcrop of rock, with shrill clarion calls announcing to all other birds that the lord of the island was abroad.

Over a thousand pairs of gulls nested on the island. I had studied their breeding habits and found a similar life history. The clutch of three eggs was laid in an open nest in late April and May. Both sexes incubated, starting immediately the first egg was laid because it was essential to be on guard against the cannibalistic habits of neighbour gulls. Average incubation period was twenty-six to twenty-seven days. Gulls are not protected by law and, although it was my policy not to interfere but simply to observe, I found it necessary to curb the increase of the powerful great black-backed gull; it was killing far too many of my beloved puffins, and storm-petrels and shearwaters. Of late years only one or two pairs of this robber gull have been allowed to rear their chicks. As for the vast colony of lesser black-backed gulls which each year returned from the south to nest on the plateau of the island, they were comparatively harmless, although expert at pulling out the nests and eggs of smaller birds they might discover; and these gulls were the principal source of our domestic egg supply – we collected about a thousand eggs each spring, for eating fresh or preserved. The cliff-nesting herring gulls were also egg-thieves, and they robbed the puffins of little fishes, as already described; but they were beautiful to watch and essentially part of the island scene the year round. Despite our collecting their eggs, they too continued to increase, to their present limit of 600 pairs.

The policy of letting nature take care of everything in her own way on a small island, and of merely observing the result, has meant that some animals have reached their upper limits of population, consistent with the availability of food and shelter. But while the land-bound rabbit and mouse are obliged to suffer that periodic fate of overpopulation – a lemming-like crash of numbers already described for the rabbit – the birds ought to be better off. They ought to be able to fly elsewhere when conditions become desperate. But do they?

One result of the many studies on Skokholm has been to show consistently that adult birds do not leave the home they have succeeded in establishing, often after years of waiting. They are like humans in this respect. It is the young things which must go out into the world and find new places to live; or else they must wait to step into dead men's shoes before they inherit a corner of the crowded earth.

This is amusingly demonstrated by the marked oyster-catchers. Solemn of mien as yeomen of the guard and as hand-somely arrayed in black and white, with scarlet sword and gaiters, they have become close friends down the years, strolling in pairs and trios near the house, watchful of their territories on the rocky knolls, but growing more and more careless of harmless bird-watchers. What were they saying when they got together and, heads bowed, sang their rapid trilling duets and threesomes? A hymn to God would not have been out of place in such a lovely environment, but the piping sounded much more like the familiar Song of Ownership: 'Ours, ours, ours! We two, we three, we two, we three! We own this plot of land! Man, man, man, go away, go away, go away! And all you other sea-pies, sea-pies, sea-pies! Go away! Ours, ours, ours!'

This was certainly the burden of their long challenging song; for if any of the would-be colonists dared to come up from the Young Oystercatchers' Club in the neutral ground along the low-water rocks they were shouted down and driven off. The oystercatchers have increased to the limit of fifty pairs, and young birds at Skokholm have to wait several years before they can find a breeding territory in the community.

The success of these splendid looking birds owes much to

161

the overgrazing by the rabbits, for oystercatchers prefer short turf and bare ground, where they find their insect and mollusc food abundantly. These conditions also suit such heathland species as larks, pipits, wheatear, lapwing and starling, and they have generally increased their breeding populations. When I first came to live on the island there were only three pairs of skylarks; today some forty pairs swell the anthem of summer song in the salty air.

Skokholm now has, I suppose, more resident birds of diverse species upon its 240 acres than any other plot of land of comparable size I can think of. There are some 80,000 adult breeding birds, which is an average of 333 to the acre – but this figure can be trebled later in the summer, with the birth of young birds and the arrival of thousands of non-breeding, sweethearting couples. In addition, during the spring and autumn migrations, hundreds of cover-loving birds, as well as heath and water birds, are caught in traps and nets, banded and released. Many of these migrants have proved to be rare wanderers to Britain; although this continuous trapping does show that some may now be considered to be of regular occurrence.

With total protection of all creatures the island is full up today. With no more room at the Inn of the Birds, but only a long queue, the island sanctuary resembles an overflowing reservoir – of wild life. I had dreamed and planned it should be such a sanctuary, but without the expectation of it becoming, possibly, the most studied small island in the world.

And what might one learn from this study, it may be asked? Man, with his supernatural power of apprehending beauty, truth and goodness, as well as evil, should find meaning as well as satisfaction from the labyrinth of practical field work and academic thought after forty years' study of the small world of Skokholm?

Yes, there has been time to stand and stare; at intervals, inwardly. If only man might learn from this complex ecological picture of a closed, overcrowded community, for Skokholm is but an epitome of the universe, a very microcosm of the world today, where thinking man is in danger of becoming as the Skokholm rabbit, debasing his existence and environment as the unthinking island cony has degraded its life and pasture – by overpopulation.

This, at least, is one lesson. Perhaps the greatest danger man faces today.

Whenever I visit the island, its marvellous beauty strikes me afresh.

Life can be sweet still, and free of care. But behind the wind in the vivid flowers, the busy pattering rabbit feet, the rich music of beating wings and calling birds, a Voice remains, too.

Why? Whither?

Appendix 1

The breeding birds of Skokholm – changes of population (pairs)

	1928	1948	1968
Storm-petrel	500	600	1,000
Manx shearwater	10,000	20,000	35,000
Buzzard	1	1	—
Oystercatcher	40	50	50
Lapwing	6	10	27
Great Black-back Gull*	31	70	5
Lesser Black-back Gull	700	350	800
Herring Gull	250	570	600
Razorbill	800	700	550
Common Guillemot	160	100	70
Puffin	20,000	8,000	1,500
Skylark	3	5	48
Raven	1	1	2
Carrion-Crow	7	7	8
Wheatear	10	20	30
Blackbird	2	—	—
Pied Wagtail	1	—	1
Dunnock	5	—	3
Meadow Pipit	45	40	36
Rock Pipit	39	40	36
Starling	—	6	30

In addition, the following species have nested irregularly: Stone-chat, Sedge-warbler, Whitethroat, Peregrine Falcon, Moorhen, Water-Rail, Mallard, Shag, Cuckoo, Little Owl, Swallow, Chough, and Kittiwake Gull.

(* a controlled population).

Appendix 2

Historical

To resume the history of the struggle to possess the little island in the tideway – from page 33 – because of its value in rabbit profits and pasturage. It seems that when his grandfather died in 1275 and Humphrey de Bohun, Earl of Hereford, came to collect his rights and dues of Skokholm, Robert de Vale stood firm and would not yield the island to him. De Bohun complained of this trespass, and in an Order (dated 21 Nov, 1275, at the Tower of London) 'Robert Duval' is required to appear before the Royal Court, then at Winchester. The King's judgement appears in the Close Rolls as follows:

1276, Jan 26. Winchester. To Nicolas son of Martin [a powerful baron then in the King's favour and warden of lands in western Wales], keeper of the island of Scugholm. Order to cause Humphrey de Bohun, Earl of Hereford, to have seisin of that island, as he lately appeared in the King's presence and sought that the king should restore the island to him as his right and his inheritance and the king thereupon caused Robert de la Vall, who likewise claimed right to the same island, to come before him at a certain day to show cause why the king should not restore the island to Humphrey, and Robert has or showed nothing for himself before the king and his council on the said day whereby any right in the island could be proved for him.

These were troubled times. The Norman barons in a hundred years of settlement had not yet altogether subjugated the wild Welsh and Irish, whose lands they had seized by force. It was necessary to retain large numbers of troops to beat off the counter-attacks. Thus armed, some barons were ready to conspire with Welsh and Irish chieftains not only against other local chieftains, but even to join with them against the King of England in a bold bid for power. Pembrokeshire was one of the most outlying baronies, for centuries subject to piratical attacks from overseas;

and from which the Normans first attacked and later conquered Ireland. Southern Pembrokeshire, with its rich level agricultural plateau and splendid harbour of Milford Haven, made a profitable base for adventures of aggrandizement. The powerful Earldom, granted to the de Clere descendants of the Duke of Normandy by the King some fifty years after the Conquest of England, not infrequently revolted against the Crown.

The islands of Skokholm, Skomer and Middleholm were included in the lands held by the Earl of Pembroke. On the treason of one or other of the Earls of Pembroke, these lands and islands were seized by the King – fortunately for the historian, since over long periods of royal ownership the revenue from the islands was recorded in the Ministerial Accounts. Thus from 1324 to 1472, an amazing series of accounts exists, to show how the islands were a source of considerable profit.

First mention of these profits appears to be in the *Inquisition post mortem* of Aymer de Valence, Earl of Pembroke, who died in 1324, without issue. The relevant extract of the document reads:

18 Edward II. No. 75, 1324. Touching the lands of the late Aymer de Valencia – Valor of the castle, town and lordship of Haverford. Total Valor £133 19s. 0½d. Pasturage of the islands of Skalmeye, Scokholm and Middelholm . . . £2 15s. 0d. Rabbit profits there . . . £14 5s. 0d.

At that time the wage of a rabbit-catcher was less than one shilling a month. The rabbit profits at £14 5s. were almost a small fortune. But why were the island rabbits so profitable? History is silent as to how this Mediterranean animal first reached the islands, but we know that the feudal system which the Normans introduced into England included many perquisites and seigneurial rights, such as maintaining dovecots, fisheries, mills and warrens. In medieval times rabbits were not universally spread over Britain as they are today, and when first introduced they were kept in enclosed warrens. The islands were ideal natural warrens, bounded by the sea, and free of ground predators such as weasels, stoats, polecats and foxes. The climate was mild, the sloping ground with its light soil excellent for dry burrows, already dug by the sea-birds.

The next document came from the Pipe Roll of Edward III, from which I copied the following details:

Receipts (Haverford and its hamlets).
Carcases and skins of rabbits caught in the islands of Schalmey, Schokolm and Middelholm, Michelmas, 1325 to January 30, 1326 . . . £13 12s.
Expenses.
Stipend of 3 ferreters . . . 12s. 3d.
Sundry expenses as follows: Salt for the aforesaid rabbit carcases,

thread for rabbit nets, boards, nail and cord for the boat used in the said islands . . . 3s. 2d.

Next, from the same Pipe Roll, is an account of what happened in the succeeding year:

Account of Robert de Penres, keeper of the castle of Haverford in Wales, by Robert Martyn, his attorney, from 30 January 1326 to 1 February 1327, the day Queen Isabella [wife of Edward II, who died in 1327] entered into the same . . . 3 May 1326 to 1 February 1327. Pasturage of the islands of Schokolme, Schalmey and Middelholme . . . £2 15s. 0d. Carcases and skins of rabbits there . . . £14 5s. 0d.

Later accounts give figures of rabbits caught, showing the value of a rabbit to vary just above one penny each in the fourteenth century; and the rabbit-catcher had only to catch three or four to pay for his weekly stipend.

There had been importations of Flemish peasants into Pembrokeshire in the twelfth century by the Norman lords, following inundations of the sea in Flanders; there had been need to recruit labourers and bondmen to replace the Welsh people who had fled from the invaders. I could picture these rabbiters on Skokholm with their broad Flemish build and faces, industriously working the winter through for a small wage, while the result of their labour was – for those days – a handsome profit for the owner, the earl or king. That was 600 years ago, and here was I, treading the same soil, perhaps using the same house!

The accounts prove that there was a house of some sort on Skokholm in this century. Probably it was little more than a shepherd's bothy, where in summer the men slept who looked after the sheep and cattle brought over from the mainland farms; and where in winter the ferreters lived, with an outhouse for the storage of wool and rabbits. Looking for evidence of this, I discovered that the present cottage seemed to be built over the foundations of an earlier building. The central room is surrounded with walls of great thickness, which were evidently the outside walls of a building at one period. The four smaller rooms (in one of which I slept) two in each wing, and a porch, were probably added much later.

The cash returns from the islands vary down the years. Sometimes the agent of the king or earl rented them to local residents, merely collecting the agreed fees, without expense of direct management. Thus from the Ministerial Accounts for 1376–7 I could extract the following interesting information:

Account of Henry Hyot, reeve of the town of Haverford, from Michaelmas 50 Edward III to Michaelmas 1 Richard II.

Pleas and Perquisites:

The agistment [grazing] of the islands of Stokeholme and Middeles-
holme 26s. 10½. The perquisites of the rabbits taken and the fisheries
there yearly 55s. 8d.

The issues of the ferry (*passagium*) . . . 6d.

These annual fees were maintained for the next four years. The
Ministerial Accounts for 1387–8 (under direct management) show
that the rabbit skins were making better profits than the carcases:

Coney returns of the islands of Skokeholme, Middelholme and Skal-
may, 1387–8: 2318 carcases, £3 17s. 3½d; 3120 skins, £8, sold to John
Wyllyam of Haverford, in gross.

Expenses: 28s. 2d. to wit: 2½ qrs. of barley for 2 ferreters in the said
islands for 21 weeks, price 6d. per bushel = 10s; 2 bushels of salt for
salting rabbit, 2s; 1 (*vanga*) shovel bought for digging out rabbits; hire
of (*oll, tripid* and *patell*) cooking utensils, for the ferreters, 6d; repair of
the house on the island of Scalmey, and of another house on the island
of Scokholm for the said ferreters as well as for the storing of the rabbits,
2s; thread for the making of rabbits nets, 4d; repair of the boat and the
purchase of 3 new oars, 6s. 10d.

This is a total of 21s. 8d.; the balance of 6s. 6d. is obviously the
stipend of the two ferreters. The discrepancy between figures for
skins and carcases is fully explained in these accounts by the notes:

3,120 carcases from the islands of Scokholm, Scalmey and Myddel-
holm. Sold 2,318. Food of 2 ferreters – 540 carcases; and food of 2
ferrets – 262 carcases.

There is also a note to these accounts showing that the sum of
£11 9s. 2d., the value of 3,000 rabbits skins of the previous winter,
charged as sold at Haverford, is respited because by the order of
Ieuan ap Gwelo and his predecessor these were conveyed to
Bristol at the Earl's expense. But at Dyneb (Tenby) they were put
in a *pluviso* (wet place), and were further wetted both on the sea
during the passage, and in a damp storehouse at Bristol, whereby
they became rotten and of no value.

The figure of 3,120 rabbits caught in the islands each winter
does not vary between 1387 and 1453. Evidently the rabbit crop
was managed with exactness to ensure a good breeding stock
remaining each spring. From my knowledge of the islands, the
numbers were probably taken in these proportions:

Skomer (Scalmey)	822 acres yielding		2,000 to	2,300	rabbits
Skokholm	240 „	„	1,000 to	750	„
Middleholm	21 „	„	120 to	70	„
	1,083 acres yielding		3,120 rabbits.		

(3,120 rabbits from 1,083 acres is roughly three rabbits from each acre. Small islands usually support more rabbits per acre than large ones.)

As we have seen (page 114) Jack and old Dick were to catch over 2,000 rabbits on Skokholm in my first winter; while my neighbour on Skomer also caught in that period more than double the figure I have suggested above for that island (as part of the total number of rabbits recorded as sold each winter in the fourteenth century).

These old records may bore the reader (if so he had better skip a few pages) but they were fascinating to me, showing how those early islanders lived chiefly on rabbits and barley. In one winter they consumed 540 rabbits for food; and in another 625 (rabbit carcases) were 'expended on the sustenance of two ferreters for 21 weeks in winter, and 252 carcases for 1 dog and 2 ferrets'. That is to say about two rabbits a day per man, and less than two a day for the three animals used for hunting the conies. I could also calculate that each rabbiter had about five pounds of barley a day for his support. Evidently a quite adequate if simple diet, and in addition, after twenty-one weeks' work, each man received 3s. in cash, equal to one farthing a day!

The cost of repairing the island houses seems to have been constant at 2s.; salt for salting down the rabbit carcases and skins was usually between 1s. 4d. and 2s. 8d.; cooking utensils hired, 4d. to 6d. Oars were a heavy expense at intervals, eight costing 6s. 2d. being required 'for the ferry boat' in 1404–5; and in the same winter 2d. was spent on a 'twyste' (a barbelé, see page 94: probably for twisting rabbits out of burrows?), and a 'scoop for removing water from the boat' is also listed.

I could enter into the lives of these men, isolated on my island, engaged in ferreting and dogging the rabbits, repairing the house, and wondering if the weather would be fine in the morning for the ferry boat to cross. The annual repairs to the boat, new oars, a scoop for bailing – all these items found an echo in my own problems and expenses in maintaining my boat, for I too was to break or lose oars at sea, and in bad weather be in dire need of the scoop for bailing out green water during my voyages, laden with the rabbits!

It was significant that these old records showed that the rabbiting terminated abruptly at the end of January; and presently I was to realize why. Early in February the shearwaters returned and began to fill the burrows. Muzzled ferrets would not work well when faced with the snapping beaks of sea-birds, (although unmuzzled these mustelids are capable of killing shearwaters, and lying up afterwards to eat them underground). Also the first young rabbits would be born at this time; the does would be in poor coat.

Although shearwaters – then known as 'harry-birds' – are not specifically mentioned, as far back as 1387–8 the sum of 6s. 8d. appears in the old accounts as revenue from the 'farm of the birds'. But pheasants did not exist in Pembrokeshire then, and the flights of duck, woodcock and snipe would have been too wild and difficult to account for revenue in this direction. Obviously sea-birds are meant. It was easy to take shearwaters in their burrows, by hand or with the barbelé. As in other isolated islands, from time immemorial, sea-birds were taken for their feathers and flesh, and their eggs regularly collected. There is a local tradition of a trade in their feathers for stuffing bed-mattress and pillow. Jack was to demonstrate to me how the fishermen used sea-birds for baiting their lobster-pots, catching them in nets set along the island cliff overnight.

Zealous attention to the farming of the sea-birds may have kept down their numbers – at any rate 6s. 8d. was the maximum paid for this perquisite, as noted in the accounts. In 1453 they fetched only 2s. let to a Fleming named Phillip Meiller. This was a winter in which a big drop in the revenue and expenses occurred: £6 15s. 11d. for rabbits sold, and 8s. 8d. for expenses.

In 1472 hunting of conies in the islands was released to the tenants by William, Earl of Pembroke, 'according to an agreement made with the Prince's Council' for the sum of forty shillings a year. In addition the agistment or grazing rights fetched another forty shillings, while *passagium* (right of ferry) was 4d. per annum. With the decline of rabbit values we find John Ogan:

tenant of the islands of Scoupholme and Scalmey, to be held by will of our lord the king from the Easter festival in the 12th year [1497] of the said king for the term of 15 years then next ensuing and to be fully ended and completed, paying 60s. each year.

The Ogans or Wogans – a famous family, which appear later in this history – made a success of their tenancy for they renewed their lease twice. Henry VIII gave the rents of the islands to Anne Boleyn when she was Marchioness of Pembroke in 1532.

In 1558 Thomas Heborne, a 'Yeoman of Their Majesties Body-guard', took it into his head to buy the remote islands for

25 years purchase at 60s. 4d. – £75 8s. 4d., payment within 14 days, the said islands lieth not near any of the king and queen majesty's honours, manors, castles, or houses whereunto their Majesties have any usual access.

Some years later the islands were in the hands of Sir John

Perrot, natural son of Henry VIII, a Pembrokeshire squire and at one time Governor of Ireland. Sir John, for having been impertinent to Queen Elizabeth, was clapped in the Tower of London, where he died in 1592. His possessions at that date were proved to include the 'Islands of Skoulkholme, Scalmage, Midelholme, and Gresholme, also the Dale'.

The Elizabethan period was one of great restlessness, with much lawless behaviour, particularly upon outlying coasts, where the spirit of privateering and piracy prevailed. The petty squires of Pembrokeshire, descendants of Norman barons, were forever engaged in feuds over property, in lawsuits, chicanery, and Star Chamber proceedings arising out of forcible entry, forcible disinheritance, extortion, theft of title-deeds, and other formidable crimes. It is very likely that this arrogant Sir John Perrot, bastard son of Good King Harry, in connivance with his avaricious henchmen, acquired the islands in the first place by illegal means. Even so it was hard to manage them profitably; there are records of pirates raiding the islands for sheep and other loot. When some of the dispersed ships of the Spanish Armada were weather-driven upon the Welsh coast the local gentry fought not against the Spaniards but with each other! One account in the Privy Council Register (for 1597) reads:

One [Spanish] ship was forced into a creek called Galtop [Goultrop, about eight miles from Skokholm]. Hereupon Mr Hugh Butler, that was in command of the trained bands in those parts, prepared six fisher boats to board the ship, but the Spaniards sent out a flag of truce and offered to send their cockboat ashore. This being perceived by one John Wogan, a gentleman of those parts, he with his brother and other associates to the number of twenty entered the ship before Mr Butler, and not only withstood him by force but wounded him in three places, while his company rifled the ship of all her goods, money and things of value.

Land was rising in value, and by the beginning of the eighteenth century it appears that Skokholm was worth at least £300, the sum raised on a mortgage by William Phillips of Haythog, a remarkable character, a barrister-at-law who was appointed sheriff of Pembrokeshire in 1646, and lived to be over a hundred years old. In the National Library of Wales is a deed of

Release dated January 18 1714/5, being a mortgage for £300 from William Phillips of Haythogg, co. Pembroke, esq., to William Allen the Younger of Gellisweek, gent., of the Island of Scowkom encompassed with the sea and Co[ntaining] by Estimacon Two Plowlands (be the same more or less) and Situated Lying and being on the West of the parishes of Marlos and Dale in the said Co. of Pembrock and reputed to be in the parish of Saint Martins in the said county of Pembrock or in what ever other parish and County the said Island is situated in.

The roll of sheriffs of Pembrokeshire shows that Hugh Butler (mentioned above) was sheriff in 1599, two years after being wounded in the affray at Galtop; and William Allen the Younger was sheriff in 1693. The latter died in 1722, aged sixty-four. He had married Elizabeth Paynter of Dale. Thus Skokholm returned after five hundred years to the possession of the occupiers of Dale Castle opposite the island, so convenient for its management.

This mortgage deed refers to houses, outhouses, buildings, barns, meadows, pasture, woods, underwoods, orchards, gardens, and 'lands as well arrable as unarrable to the said Island belonging', but this was the invariable phraseology of legal instruments of this period. We can be sure that there were no woods thereon at this time, but cannot be sure that the present range of farm buildings were not already existing at this date – around 1700, and certainly by 1760. Up to that time there was at least the shepherd-warrener's bothy mentioned in the fourteenth century deeds, but in what state of repair it was before the present buildings were erected I could not discover.

It was a period of prospering agriculture and rising farm prices and rents, evidence for which I presently found in an account of the island by Richard Fenton, barrister and man of letters, who spent much time investigating the antiquities of his native Pembrokeshire. He was born in the county in 1747 and died there in 1821, having seen his bulky volume, *A Historical Tour through Pembrokeshire*, fruit of many years research, published in 1811. While living in London Fenton had enjoyed the friendship of Dr Samuel Johnson, Oliver Goldsmith, David Garrick, Edmund Burke, Joshua Reynolds, and other famous men. At home he toured the county, and stayed with local squires – the *petite noblesse de campagne* (he had married a beautiful French aristocrat, and used her language freely). At the time of visiting Dale, about 1800, he stayed at the castle there with John Lloyd, a high sheriff of the county, who had married (1776) the heiress of Dale and Skokholm, Elinor, great grand-daughter of William Allen the Younger (above).

Fenton must have seen Skokholm from Dale, but evidently did not cross to the island. However, in his *Tour*, he gives the best account of that period we yet have of Skokholm:

My friend, Mr J. Lloyd, has kindly supplied me with the following description of Skokholm, which I add in his words, for I cannot improve them:

'Skokham is mine in right of my wife. It is now rented to a tenant of the name of Stewart for £100 per annum. If permitted to exist, it would be over-run with rabbits which I would not chuse, as it is well supplied with pasture and arable land and has several springs of fine fresh water. I held it in my own hands for three years together, and had a dairy of eight or nine cows on it. I had also oats and barley growing in the fields thereon at the same time, and mowed a part cropped with rye grass and clover which had been sown for the horses. However, little winter fodder was required because I had not nearly stocked the island with horses and cattle, so that the fog of grass kept my stock in good ordinary style during the winter months, for the snow lies but a short time on it, on account, I imagine, of being surrounded by the sea.

'It has here and there rocks interspersed, which are upright or a little shelving, and insulated, if I may use the term, throughout the Island, which afford shelter to the cattle and sheep, whenever the stormy winds set in from one side or other of the isle. In one rainy summer, when I held it in my own hands, the herbage was over-run with white clover.

'There is a dwelling house on it, built by a gentleman who held it before me, built after a whimsical manner, which has a small beast house and a dairy, with stables besides.

'When servants in charge of the farm on the Island, or other persons stand in need of supplies, or wish to hold communication with the mainland, they signal by making dense smoke with damp straw or fern, which grow upon many parts of the isle, and it is answered by sending in a boat from persons who look out for such signals, who after ascertaining the requirements supply what is wanted.

'There are two landing places on the Island, which are called the North and South Havens, and it must be bad weather indeed when the isle is not accessible on one side or the other, and in either, or both of these Havens places might be made to haul up a boat by means of tackle out of reach of any sea, be it ever so tempestuous.

'At low water on the North side a considerable quantity of sand may be brought up for manuring the land, and lime ready burnt may be brought there in bags or casks for any purpose required. Mr Allen, my wife's father, put some deer upon it, and when I held it in my hands I replenished them with some fawns, given to me by Lord Milford. They did not breed well, however, but the deer grew extremely fat, and were remarkably fine flavoured. At the christening of my late departed eldest son [born 1777, died 1805], I killed a buck, the venison of which was judged by the large company assembled never to have been equalled in Pembrokeshire. My family increasing, I found it necessary to rent out the Island, and as the tenant then was continually teasing me about the damage the deer did him, I gave him leave to destroy them all, which he did not fail to do. If these few particulars about Skokham should be worth your adopting, you are welcome to them.

'I forgot to mention that there is a bog of peat or turf on Skokham Island of about five or six acres, which makes good firing, and that I have had the whole Island measured, and it contains 202 acres 2 roods and 2 perches. It stands about five miles from St Ann's Head at the entrance to Milford Haven, and about three miles from Jack's Sound, the entrance into St Bride's Bay on which is a landing place for boats, called Martin's Haven, from whence cattle and live stock are more frequently carried than from Milford Haven. It is extra parochial, and therefore pays no parish rates or tythes whatever, although taken to be part of the County of Pembroke.'

This letter must have been written shortly after the death in 1805 of Lloyd's eldest son, John Allen Lloyd. It is a most helpful description, and accurate enough (except in the measurement of the island, which, when I took it over, was declared to be just over 242 acres) to enable me to understand how that early stock and arable farm was managed by the gentleman owner or tenant and his servants.

There is no reference to the sea-birds, and evidently they were not plentiful enough to warrant mention as a source of revenue or sport.

Reference to the house as built in a whimsical manner is understandable to any who has seen it today, practically unaltered from its appearance then; for the steep roof is brought down to within five feet of the ground on the north and south sides, giving it an unusual wind-resistant, almost tent-like, form as it rests snugly sheltered from the prevailing south-westerly gales close to the rocky hillock of the shearwater knoll.

As there was no winch or tackle to haul up a boat, the farmer and his family were dependent on the service of boats from the mainland. But later the retired sea-captain Henry Edward Harrison became tenant, who, so to speak, still kept one leg in the sea by maintaining his own boat on Skokholm. He had five daughters, three of whom were on the island when Thomas Marriott visited it. Marriot wrote to me (from Australia):

My home at that time was on the north shore of Milford Haven and as a young man I possessed an 18ft whaleboat in which I cruised round the coast as far south as Tenby. We camped on Skokholm in August 1878, before I went to the South African Diamond Fields in 1879 (where I met Cecil Rhodes). Our tent was a military Bell tent and there were five of us in the party. We had a very pleasant time, and found the Harrison family very kind and hospitable.

Mr Harrison was a retired sea captain and worked the farm on the Island growing barley, potatoes and vegetables. He had three daughters (the one I remember best was named Ellen, who appeared to be the eldest) who assisted in working the farm and milked several cows. I think they employed a farm hand as well. I remember being told by Mr Harrison that he paid the rent with the rabbits he caught on the Island. In those days the farm house and outbuildings and fences were in good order and repair. I remember assisting in getting the harvest in while there. Before I left the Island in my boat, two of my friends left in a

Marloes fishing boat for the mainland. Then in the following week I left with two others to row to Milford Haven but owing to a strong tide against us we could not reach St Ann's Head and landed at a little place shown on the chart (near Gateholm Stack) where we climbed the cliffs and spent the night in a ruined cottage.

I had already met the sole surviving daughter of Captain Harrison, who had married a Marloes fisherman, and was living in the village. Mrs Folland at that moment was a charming old lady of seventy-eight, whose memory of her childhood life on Skokholm was still sound. She remembered that her father had much improved the South Haven landing place, cleaning up the beach there sufficiently to permit small sailing ships (ketches of 30 tons burthen) in fine weather to come in at high tide, and be beached over low water for loading corn, or unloading supplies, chiefly limestone (and anthracite for burning the stone) for burning and spreading on the fields. It seems that the corn (barley and oats) grown on the salty island soil was noted for its purity and quality, and much in demand for seed on mainland farms.

Mrs Folland could not remember if her father had built the neat little lime-kiln just above the harbour, still in perfect shape, but nowadays used only by the storm-petrels which nest in its crannies and in the heap of unused lime stones beside it. But she remembered that he had made a broad cart-track through the solid rock so that a horse and cart could be backed right down to the topmost landing step, and thus cargoes could be loaded or unloaded direct between ship and cart by the ship's winch and yard-arm, expeditiously and sailor fashion.

It was a sad day for the island farming when her father died there in 1881, his son unwilling to follow his example; and no tenant was found subsequently who was able and prepared to carry on the tradition he had established. It was a moment of agricultural depression, when thousands of young farmers and their families were emigrating to America and the colonies abroad. Rents were falling. Farmers on the mainland were prepared to graze their stock, but not to live, on the island. Gradually the unoccupied, neglected buildings, under the blows of winter storms, lost their roofs.

In 1905 the staunch Fleming, Edwards of Orlandon, attempted a restoration. He had already told me much – retrospectively – about the happy days which he and his wife had enjoyed there. According to local gossip his natural tenacity had earned him the title of Bulldog. But although he had boasted to me of the splendid farm he had maintained there, and its superlative yield of crops, colts, and dairy produce, according to my man Jack, and others even more critical, Bulldog was given to religious meditation, had taken life very easily, and done little but catch rabbits and fish. But subsequently he had made quite a useful lot of money supplying horses and transport when Trinity House began to build a light-house at the western end of Skokholm. This was completed about the time of the outbreak of war in 1914, and meanwhile Bulldog had removed himself and his farm to Orlandon.

From that time onwards Skokholm was left to the rabbit-catchers in winter, who tore more holes in the stone-banked hedges so that the article of their trade might flourish better; and to the fishermen in the summer, who set their long-nets under the cliffs to obtain cocklollies (shearwaters) and sea-parrots (puffins) with which to bait their fishing pots.

Such was the state of the island when I took possession in that first and stormy October. Stormy but not lonely. I saw friendli-ness everywhere, in its beautiful rocks, its marvellous bird life, and in its sense of history, its feeling of long use by man far back into its Norse naming, its Norman warreners, its recent farming by sea-captain Harrison.

O, a goodly, vivid place to be!